The Business of Health

The Business of Health

The Role of Competition, Markets, and Regulation

Robert L. Ohsfeldt
and
John E. Schneider

The AEI Press

Publisher for the American Enterprise Institute

WASHINGTON, D.C.

Distributed to the Trade by National Book Network, 15200 NBN Way, Blue Ridge Summit, PA 17214. To order call toll free 1-800-462-6420 or 1-717-794-3800. For all other inquiries please contact the AEI Press, 1150 Seventeenth Street, N.W., Washington, D.C. 20036 or call 1-800-862-5801.

Library of Congress Cataloging-in-Publication Data
Ohsfeldt, Robert L.
    The business of health : the role of competition, markets, and regula-
tion / Robert L. Ohsfeldt and John E. Schneider.
        p cm
    Includes bibliographical references and index.
    ISBN-13: 978-0-8447-4240-3
    ISBN-10: 0-8447-4240-6
    1. Medical economics. 2. Health services administration.
I. Schneider, John E. II. Title.
    [DNLM: 1. Economic Competition—United States. 2. Health Care
Sector—organization & administration—United States. 3. Drug Indus-
try—economics—United States. 4. Economics, Hospital—organization
& administration—United States. 5. Health Policy—economics—United
States. 6. Insurance, Health—economics—United States.   W 74 AA1
O38b 2006]
RA410.O357 2006
362.1068—dc22

                                                            2006021676

11 10 09 08 07 06   1 2 3 4 5 6

Printed in the United States of America

*Robert Ohsfeldt dedicates this book
to Erika, Michael, and Britta*

*John Schneider dedicates this book
to Audrey and Lena*

Contents

List of Illustrations

TABLES

Acknowledgments

Dr. Schneider is supported by a Merit Review Entry Program Award and an Investigator Initiated Award from the Health Services Research and Development Service, Veterans Health Administration, Department of Veterans Affairs.

The authors would like to acknowledge the very helpful contributions to and reviews or critiques of all or parts of the manuscript by Jack Calfee, Michael A. Morrisey, Bennet A. Zelner, Thomas R. Miller, Martin Gaynor, James C. Robinson, Steve Culler, Leslie A. Sprout, Alan Pierrot, Randy Fenninger, Molly Gutierrez, Regina Herzlinger, Brian Dulisse, Walter Zelman, Maureen O'Haren, and Brian Kaskie. Valuable research assistance was provided by Yang Lei, Pengxiang Li, Eric Mooss, Erika Ohsfeldt, Kaley Sholes, Bobbi Buckner Bentz, Janet Benton, Alexis Barbour, and Lauren Tucker Huber. We would also like to thank Robert Helms at AEI for his editorial guidance and patience through the writing process.

Portions of chapters 1 and 5 have been adapted from Ohsfeldt (2004). The discussion in chapter 2 devoted to single-payer health coverage initiatives is based on research that received partial support from the California Association of Health Underwriters. Chapter 3 is based on research that received partial support from the American Surgical Hospital Association and the South Dakota Association of Specialty Care Providers. Chapter 4 is based on research that was partially supported by a grant to John Schneider from the University of Iowa Carver College of Medicine and College of Public Health New Investigator Research Award (January 2002).

Introduction

There is something of a consensus among health policy experts, though it is less than unanimous, that the U.S. health care system represents a prime example of the wrong way to organize and finance a health-care delivery system. The World Health Organization (WHO) has ranked the performance of the U.S. health system thirty-seventh out of 191 member countries, approximately equal in performance to those of Chile, Costa Rica, Cuba, Dominica, and Slovenia, and well behind France (ranked first) and Italy (ranked second).[1] The primary factor contributing to this relatively poor ranking is assignment by the WHO of demerits for a lack of fairness in financing in the U.S. system (that is, coexistence of the well-insured and uninsured), coupled with mediocre population health outcomes (such as less than stellar life expectancy at birth), despite high levels of spending.

The Organization for Economic Cooperation and Development (OECD) is similarly unimpressed in its assessment of U.S. health care system performance. In an OECD review, Docteur, Suppanz, and Woo conclude it is "doubtful that mere marginal reforms could adequately deal with the problems [of] soaring costs, low value for money relative to population health status and unsatisfactory coverage and access to health services."[2] They do acknowledge that "fundamental reform lacks sufficient political support" in part because "the U.S. system is seen *domestically* to have considerable advantages" (emphasis added).

Numerous ills of the U.S. system also have been characterized in several recent books. Many of the critics cite the apparently adverse effects of services being provided by private organizations seeking profit rather than serving the public. For example, Mueller, in *As Sick as It Gets*, laments that the system is "contaminated by its focus on money and its exploitation of the massive cash flow that modern medical technology has created. Its

1

mission should be to maximize the well-being and health of every individual and our society as a whole."[3] In *Critical Condition*, Bartlett and Steele complain that "as long as Washington remains wedded to the illusion that market-based medicine will cure health care's woes, tens of billions of dollars per year will vanish into waste, inefficiency, fraud, and profits to companies that make money by denying care."[4] Kassirer asserts in *On the Take* that health care providers have been corrupted by profit-seeking producers of prescription drugs and devices, caring too much about what is good for these producers and not enough about what is good for their patients.[5] In a similar vein, Abramson in *Overdosed America* describes a "transformation of medical science from a public good whose purpose is to improve health into a commodity whose primary function is to maximize financial returns." He concludes that, as a result, "the commercialization of medicine [is not] just causing doctors to prescribe unnecessary drugs and procedures [but is] actually subverting the quality of medical care."[6]

Another common theme in these critiques is the needless complexity of the U.S. system, with its diffuse sources of funding and resulting multiplicity of payment systems and policies. In *Oxymorons*, Kleinke laments that the fragmented sources of financing and the plethora of health plans create "an administrative fiasco for health insurers that has drained billions of health insurance dollars otherwise marked for health care." This fragmentation means that "the kind of care you receive in [the United States] has less to do with how sick you are and more to do with the kind of insurance you carry." In Kleinke's view, federalism compounds the problem: "The arbitrary state versus federal bifurcation of health plan regulation, played out state by state—and all of the extra administrative cost, inefficiency, and Chaos Factor they generate—is not only stupid but futile."[7]

What can be done to correct these deficiencies in the U.S. system? In Mueller's vision, the solution entails (among other things) banning for-profit hospitals and health insurance providers. Bartlett and Steele contend that a government-managed, single-payer system would cure what ails the U.S. system, by improving access to needed care while reducing the resources wasted on the promotion of unnecessary care by profit-seeking service providers and the shifting of payment responsibility by profit-seeking insurers.[8]

In some cases, critics of the U.S. health system seem to compare it to a hypothetical nirvana state, where issues of resource scarcity, moral hazard, adverse selection, and imperfect information play a minor role. But, more often, the comparisons are to health systems in other developed nations, systems thought to produce superior outcomes at a lower cost. The common refrain is, "If only the United States could adopt a health system more like Canada's [or Germany's, or whatever health system the critic finds attractive], we, too, could achieve better health outcomes at lower cost." As noted, the culprit thought to be responsible for the relatively mediocre performance of the U.S. health care system is typically some combination of destructive competition and for-profit medicine or corporate greed, or, more generally, the "business model" of health care. The implication is that health system performance in the United States would be enhanced substantially if the adverse impact of the business model could be purged by government, either through direct ownership of the system or rigorous controls on expenditures through comprehensive, administered pricing systems or global budget caps.

On the other side of the argument are those who interpret the available evidence on system performance to imply, more generally, that on balance consumers would benefit if market forces were encouraged (or at least permitted). These authors cite evidence that market-oriented incentives generate better outcomes than less competitive alternatives within many of the components of the health care system. Examples of these perspectives are David Cutler's *Your Money or Your Life*, David Dranove's *From Marcus Welby to Managed Care*, James Robinson's *The Corporate Practice of Medicine*, *Market Driven Health Care* and related research by Regina Herzlinger, and Cannon and Tanner's *Healthy Competition*.[9] These authors acknowledge progress but conclude there is ample room for improvement in the U.S. health care system. Unlike the largely negative accounts of the critics, however, they envision improvements as primarily a challenge of harnessing the benefits of markets while extending coordinated support through all levels of government for those who fall between the market's cracks, mainly the uninsured and indigent and the providers who disproportionately serve them. The challenge, as described by a recent report by the U.S. Federal Trade Commission and the Department of Justice, is to encourage the development of a health care system that takes full advantage of the cost and quality benefits of competition while employing efficient regulatory and redistributive policies to aid those who, for a variety of reasons, cannot share in the benefits of competition.[10]

In this book, we review the role of profit-seeking and competition in health care. Chapter 1 provides an overview of U.S. health system performance in comparison with systems in other developed countries. Specifically, we take a close look at the assertion that U.S. health care expenditures are excessive, and that system performance is poor. Data from the OECD are used to show how the United States aligns with other high-income developed countries. Our main contentions are that, although market and government imperfections exist, the U.S. health care system does not produce clearly excessive expenditures, nor does it woefully underperform systems in other developed countries.

Chapter 2 considers the question whether profit-seeking behavior in health care is inappropriate, as many market critics have averred. We review the evidence and reach the general conclusion that—consistent with economic theory—profit-seeking behavior is not antithetical to good health care.

The profit-seeking chapter sets the stage for the three chapters that follow (3–5), which discuss specific aspects of profit-seeking as it relates to the case of specialty hospitals, managed care reform, and direct-to-consumer prescription drug marketing, respectively. Throughout the book we examine the proposition that profit-seeking on the part of providers of health services contributes to excess spending or adversely affects the health of the public, and the corollary proposition that government ownership or control of service provision reduces costs and improves health outcomes. Our conclusion offers some closing remarks and a discussion of policy implications.

1

U.S. Health System Performance:
An International Perspective

According to data collected by the Organization for Economic Cooperation and Development, the United States spends more on health care than any other OECD country, measured either as health spending per capita (adjusted for purchasing power parity)[1] or as a percentage of gross domestic product (GDP). This fact, coupled with the lack of correspondent superlative health outcomes—at least as indicated by broad population-level health measures—generally is interpreted as providing proof of the inherent inefficiency of the U.S. system. In turn, this apparent inefficiency often is attributed to wasteful duplication of facilities and administrative infrastructure (due to a lack of centralization), wasteful competition among health service providers, and the provision of unnecessary services by profit-seeking providers.

To begin our discussion, we focus first on the fundamental question: Does the U.S. health system significantly underperform health systems in other high-income developed countries? We suggest that the factual basis for this common conclusion may be open to interpretation. In the remainder of the chapter, we focus on three aspects of underperformance: excessive expenditures, mediocre health outcomes, and inequitable access to care.

Health Expenditures

Clearly, definitional complexities abound in any crossnational comparisons of "health care" spending, but let us take it as a given that per-capita spending on health care is greater in the United States than any other OECD country. Let us also take it as a given that per-capita GDP, adjusted for purchasing power parity, generally has been greater in the United States than in any other OECD country (excluding tiny Luxembourg).[2] Under these circumstances, one would expect the higher GDP in the United States to translate into higher health care spending relative to other OECD countries, because health care is a "normal" good. Individuals choose to consume more of a normal good as income rises.

One method to summarize the association between GDP per capita and health spending per capita is a regression model, where a simple mathematical relationship between per-capita health spending and GDP that best "fits" the data is identified. A graphic based on a linear model specification for the regression analysis often has been employed to illustrate the magnitude of excessive health spending in the United States. A recent example is presented by Docteur, Suppanz, and Woo[3] and is replicated in figure 1-1, based on a linear regression model using data for all OECD countries (except Luxembourg) for 2000.[4] In the figure, the positions of three specific OECD countries are highlighted by labels: the United States (USA), Sweden (SWE), and Turkey (TUR). The United States represents the maximum value of both health spending and GDP per capita in the OECD sample, while Turkey represents the minimum value of both. In contrast, the values of health spending and GDP per capita for Sweden are both relatively near the OECD sample mean.

The result illustrated in figure 1-1 indicates a strikingly large difference between actual and predicted health spending per capita for the United States (referred to as the U.S. "residual"). The common interpretation of this result is that it demonstrates not only that the United States spends more on health care per capita than any other OECD country, but it spends much more than expected even given higher per-capita GDP in the United States. In other words, health spending in the United States appears to be substantially greater than expected, even after accounting for the impact of higher income on health spending. Thus, this substantial excess spending must be attributable to other factors, such as waste and inefficiency.

At this point, however, it might be helpful to recall that under the least-squares criterion for best fit used in standard regression analysis, the estimated regression coefficients are those that minimize the sum of the squared

FIGURE 1-1

FITTED REGRESSION LINE FOR HEALTH EXPENDITURES PER CAPITA AND
GDP PER CAPITA, OECD COUNTRIES, 2000: LINEAR SPECIFICATION[1]

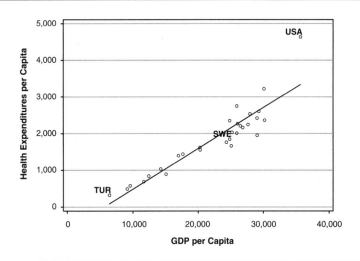

SOURCE: Authors' analysis of OECD data.
NOTE: 1. Linear Regression: HealthExpPC = −628.74 + 0.1113 GDPPC, R^2 = 0.846

residuals across all observations in the sample. The specific coefficients providing the best fit for the data thus are influenced by where in the sample distribution most of the data reside. For a sample following a "normal" distribution, about two-thirds will reside within one standard deviation of the mean. By design, the regression model will, in general, provide a better fit in the neighborhood of a sample distribution where data are dense, compared to portions of the sample distribution where data are sparse. Thus, for a particular observation in a "sparse" region of the sample distribution, the fit of the regression model will tend to be more sensitive to changes in the assumed functional form, or "shape," of the regression line than for a particular observation in a dense region of the sample.

In this context, it should be noted that values for health spending and GDP per capita for the United States clearly are not clustered near OECD countries with similar values (see figure 1-1). Indeed, as mentioned above, the United States represents the extreme value for both health spending per

FIGURE 1-2

FITTED REGRESSION LINE FOR HEALTH EXPENDITURES PER CAPITA AND GDP PER CAPITA, OECD COUNTRIES, 2000: SEMILOG SPECIFICATION[1]

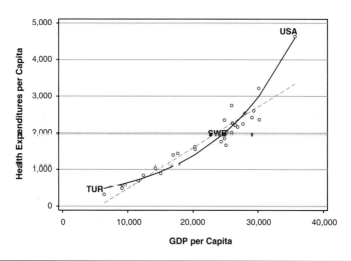

SOURCE: Authors' analysis of OECD data.

NOTE: 1. Semilog Regression: log (HealthExpPC) = 5.66 + 7.7E-05 GDPPC, R^2 = 0.926

capita and GDP per capita in the OECD sample for 2000. Thus, the United States is positioned in a "sparse" region of the sample distribution. As a result, the size of the estimated U.S. residual in a regression model can be very sensitive to the choice of the shape assumption for the regression line. In contrast, Sweden is positioned in a relatively dense portion of the OECD sample distribution. As such, one might expect estimated residuals for Sweden to exhibit comparatively less sensitivity to the shape assumption used for the regression analysis.

To illustrate this point, consider a common variant of a linear regression model specification: a semilog model. In a semilog model, the dependent variable (in this case health spending per capita) is transformed into its natural logarithm. An analogous graphic for the semilog regression model is provided in figure 1-2.[5] Note that, in stark contrast to figure 1-1, the U.S. residual in this case is close to zero, and clearly smaller than the residual value for many other OECD countries.

FIGURE 1-3

FITTED REGRESSION LINE FOR HEALTH EXPENDITURES PER CAPITA AND
GDP PER CAPITA, OECD COUNTRIES, 2000: LOG-LOG SPECIFICATION[1]

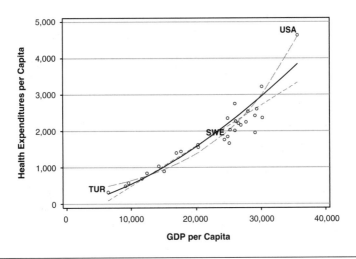

SOURCE: Authors' analysis of OECD data.
NOTE: 1. Log-log Regression: log (HealthExpPC) = –6.35 + 1.38 Log(GDPPC), R^2 = 0.954

Of course, the small U.S. residual for the semilog model does not prove
that the level of health spending is about what one should expect given
GDP in the United States, any more than the large residual in the linear
model proves U.S. health spending is substantially greater than expected.
These are but two of any number of possible assumptions for the shape of
the regression line. Indeed, as shown in figure 1-3, a loglinear model
(where both per-capita health spending and GDP are transformed to loga-
rithms) produces an estimated U.S. residual of a more intermediate magnitude. A quadratic model specification (where GDP per capita and its square
are used to predict health spending) produces a relatively "small" positive
residual, whereas a cubic regression model specification (where GDP per
capita, its square, and its cubed values are used to predict health spending)
produces an estimated U.S. residual that is *negative*. Thus, the size of the
estimated U.S. residual is very sensitive to the assumed shape of the regression line.[6] By contrast, for countries with per-capita health spending and

GDP near that of many other OECD countries (for example, Sweden), the estimated residuals are small in all of these alternative regression model shape specifications.

The fundamental point of our discussion is that quantifying the extent of excessive health spending in the United States from a residual value in a regression model is inherently problematic, given that the answer depends on an essentially arbitrary choice of shape for the regression line. However, in most model specifications, the estimated U.S. residual is positive and not small. This is especially evident when this exercise is replicated with the most recent OECD data.[7] Thus, it seems unlikely that higher rates of health spending in the United States can be explained by higher income alone. Although it would be difficult to quantify with any degree of precision the extent to which the level of spending is greater than expected spending, it probably is safe to assume it is at least somewhat higher than expected relative to other high-income developed countries. If so, what factors, other than waste and inefficiency, might explain the higher expenditures?

One possibility relates to differences in access to discretionary health care services across countries. The use of such services will tend to increase with income, in the absence of nonmarket constraints. However, health systems in many high-income OECD countries restrict access to services deemed to be not medically necessary. Residents of these high-income countries might be willing to spend more on discretionary health care services if their governments helped them to pay for them, or allowed such services to be purchased at all. Revealed preference suggests that consumers place some value on the use of these services, even if they have no particularly obvious impact on health outcomes such as life expectancy. In the absence of access constraints other than price, health spending in high-income countries might be closer to U.S. spending levels.

Another possible source of higher cost is seemingly redundant capacity in the U.S. system, in the form of underutilized capital equipment or the coexistence of similar providers or health plans within a particular market area. However, greater capacity contributes to shorter waiting times,[8] which is likely to have some value to consumers even if it does not directly translate into better health outcomes. Greater capacity is also useful in the event of unexpected spikes in demand for medical services, such as those caused by disease outbreaks, natural disasters, or large-scale accidents.[9] Likewise, the ability to choose between two seemingly similar products may have value to consumers, even if it does not improve health.

Using a non–health-related analogy for excess capacity, suppose that there are two gas stations on opposite corners of an intersection. Suppose further that, at many times over the course of the day, few if any consumers use the gas pumps at either station. Does this indicate an "excess capacity" of gas stations at the intersection? Although some urban planners might answer that question in the affirmative, most consumers recognize on an intuitive level that there are distinct advantages to this situation. The first is that the likely waiting time required to fill their gas tanks at the time most convenient for them to do so is reduced. The second is that the existence of two competing vendors of gasoline undoubtedly translates into lower prices and a higher quality of service than they would have encountered in the absence of competition. The advantages of seemingly redundant capacity are also evident in the supply-chain contracting practices of Japanese automobile manufacturers, who typically contract with multiple parts-suppliers even if capacity exceeds production needs.[10] The rationale is that maintaining at least two viable parts-suppliers fosters competition and reduces the uncertainty associated with unanticipated increases in final-product demand.

Consumers also may attach value to seemingly irrelevant differences in product characteristics, and may be willing to pay a premium for them. To use another non–health-related analogy, suppose an objective observer notes that there are few functional differences between a Toyota Camry and a Honda Accord. Would the welfare of car buyers be improved if apparently meaningless choices of this sort could be eliminated? Those who would answer in the affirmative argue that savings could be achieved by eliminating duplicative product development effort, by improving efficiency in production through scale economies, and by reducing unnecessary marketing and sales costs. However, in the absence of competition between Honda and Toyota (and Ford and Nissan and . . .), it is doubtful that a single car manufacturer would have been driven to the sorts of innovations required over time to produce a car equal in quality to either an Accord or a Camry.

In the U.S. health system, recent trends in insurance markets indicate a clear preference for plans with fewer restrictions on patient choice.[11] This suggests that consumers are willing to pay some positive value for choice. The extent of the willingness to pay for subtle differences in health plan characteristics affecting choice is likely to be exaggerated by tax incentives that insulate consumers from cost differences in employer-sponsored health insurance options. The recent movement by employers toward defined-contribution health benefits represents an effort to address this phenomenon.

While a preference for more discretionary services and choice may in part explain higher levels of health spending in the United States, a more basic explanation relates to differences in the prices of inputs used to produce health care.[12] The popular press has directed considerable attention to the higher prices of certain brand-name prescription drugs in the United States than in Canada and other developed countries. But most inputs used to produce health care services also have higher prices in the United States than in Canada. For example, physicians, nurses, and other skilled, hospital-based employees in the United States earn more than their counterparts in Canada.[13] Thus, even if residents of the two countries consumed exactly the same quantities of health services, expenditures per capita would be higher in the United States, even after adjusting for economy-wide differences in price levels using a total purchasing power parity index.

The usual interpretation of the higher prices for brand-name drugs in the United States is that the prescription drug prices here are too high, but some (mainly for generics) are, in fact, lower than in Canada. Whether prices on average are higher or lower depends on the choice of consumption weights used to define "average"—a classic index number problem.[14] It is commonly assumed that the higher prices for brand-name drugs in the United States enable drug manufacturers to sell their products at lower prices in other high-income developed countries, while retaining an overall return on investment sufficient to finance research and development for new products. If this is the case, reducing cross-subsidization would reduce U.S. health spending and increase health spending in other high-income OECD countries.[15] However, a more likely explanation for the pattern of cross-national prices is price discrimination, where a monopolist charges more in less price-sensitive markets. If so, as Morrisey explains in the context of hospital pricing, reducing the extent of price controls in other high-income countries would not necessarily result in a reduction in U.S. prices, nor would the imposition of controls in the United States cause price increases in other countries.[16]

Some might contend that significant reductions in U.S. health spending could be achieved by cutting payments to providers of health services. Indeed, simply reducing the earnings of physicians and other skilled health-sector labor in the United States to Canadian levels would (in a static model) eliminate a substantial portion of the alleged excess in U.S. health care expenditures. But are the incomes of physicians and other skilled health workers in the United States really too high? With the possible exception of some subspecialties, the return on investment in medical education is pretty much in line with the rates of return on education for other professional occupations, such as attorney or business executive.[17] The health sector must compete with other sectors for labor, so it is doubtful that physicians' incomes could be reduced substantially without adversely affecting the supply of physician services. Likewise, significantly reducing the wages of nurses would almost certainly exacerbate the current nursing shortage.

While it is plausible to suggest that higher levels of U.S. health spending can be explained in part by higher input prices and higher levels of discretionary health care utilization, waste and inefficiency undoubtedly also play a role. However, a practical difficulty in measuring the contribution of waste and inefficiency to excess health spending is the definition of terms. Labeling a particular input or output as waste requires an explicit differentiation between that which is useful and that which is not. Those who contend that waste and inefficiency are significant contributors to excess health spending in the United States often point to administrative costs as a salient metric.[18]

There are two fundamental problems with treating administrative costs as a proxy for waste. First, as the recent experiences with Enron, Health-South, and WorldCom have amply demonstrated, accountants have a fair amount of discretion over the allocation of costs to different functions within an organization. Financial statements are, in essence, report cards that organizations generate for specific audiences to judge their performance. Tax-exempt organizations have as a mission the provision of service; thus, they have an incentive to use their discretion to maximize their reported levels of expenditures for services and minimize costs attributed to administration or overhead in reports to donors and regulators. In contrast, the audience for the financial statements produced by for-profit organizations in general will tend to focus on the difference between total revenue and total costs; the share of costs classified as administrative at any point in time is not an especially salient issue. This makes any meaningful comparison of administrative costs across organizations with very different missions inherently difficult.[19] Thus, a study finding that the share of total costs classified as administrative in a tax-exempt organization tends to be lower than in a for-profit organization[20] has no particularly meaningful interpretation.

Second, defining administrative costs as waste requires the assumption that administration (which includes management) is essentially a superfluous function that produces nothing of value. Yet a managerial function is essential to the operation of any organization, and can serve to ensure access to needed services while reducing utilization of less valuable ones.[21] This has obvious implications for the "administration is waste" construct. For example, Danzon argues that the Canadian health system makes very limited use of patient or provider financial incentives or utilization management mechanisms to avoid unnecessary care.[22] The result is queues for "free" services,[23] which impose substantial costs on health care consumers. In contrast, Kahn and colleagues, using data from Milliman USA, found that more than one-third (3.7 percentage points) of the total administrative costs of commercial health insurance plans in California (9.9 percent of premiums) was attributed to customer service, information systems, and major clinical activities, such as case management.[24] Presumably, these functions serve to make needed services available in a convenient and timely manner for health plan members. Thus, simply comparing self-reported costs for management effort across different types of organizations in different health systems, and asserting that this is a valid measure of waste, fails to provide any useful evidence concerning comparative efficiency.

The liability environment in the United States also is frequently cited as a potential contributor to excessive health spending.[25] Kessler and McClellan conclude that various forms of tort reform enacted from 1984 to 1990 reduced the costs of health care without any discernable impact on patient outcomes.[26] Thus, a relatively tort-friendly legal environment seems to induce physicians to provide excessive care (practice "defensive medicine") in the hope that doing so will reduce their liability exposure. By one estimate, tort reform could reduce total medical care expenditures in the United States by 5–9 percent per year, or $70 billion to $140 billion in 2003.[27]

Other studies find a less dramatic effect of liability on health care costs. Anderson and colleagues conclude that medical liability claims paid per

FIGURE 1-4

GROWTH IN HEALTH SPENDING PER CAPITA (PPP$),
SELECTED OECD COUNTRIES, 1980–99

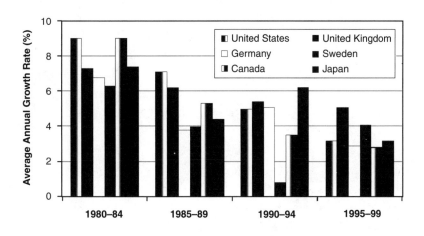

SOURCE: Organization for Economic Cooperation and Development (2003).

capita are only modestly higher in the United States than in other high-income developed countries.[28] Morrisey, Kilgore, and Nelson find modest effects of tort reform on employer health insurance premiums, which presumably reflect the impact of reforms on both liability insurance rates and the liability-induced provision of excess service.[29] Measuring the cost impact of defensive medicine is inherently problematic,[30] but, based on the available evidence, it would be difficult to conclude with any reasonable degree of certainty that the liability environment is a major contributor to differentially higher health spending in the United States. Nonetheless, it seems clear that effective tort reform would reduce spending on health care at least modestly, and might be socially beneficial for other reasons.[31]

Although the *level* of health spending in the United States is consistently higher than in any other OECD country, the rate of *growth* in spending here has not been markedly greater than in other high-income countries. As illustrated in figure 1-4, many other health systems have experienced growth in spending similar to that observed in the United States. This similarity exists despite the higher rate of growth in GDP in the United

States, and despite the administered pricing, centralized global budgeting, access restrictions, and other cost-control measures often employed in other systems. The surprisingly similar trend in expenditure growth is most likely attributable to common trends across developed countries, such as aging of the population. Whatever the defects of the U.S. system, if they contribute to an unusually high level of spending, they cannot also be said to contribute to unusually high rates of growth in spending.

Health Outcomes

Given that the United States spends more on health care than other developed countries, it might be reasonable to expect its health care system to produce outcomes superior to those of systems spending less. A common theme among those expounding on mediocre U.S. health outcomes relates to the fair-to-middling values for the United States among several broad, population-level measures of health, relative to other high-income developed countries. The most commonly used measures are life expectancy or healthy (quality-adjusted) life expectancy at birth or specific ages, and infant or child mortality rates (see examples in table 1-1). Taken at face value, these data provide very little indication that higher health spending translates into better health outcomes in the United States. This result generally is interpreted as further evidence that much of the additional health expenditure in the United States is wasted—that is, not spent on something that creates value as measured by these common indicators.

These population-health outcomes data for the United States clearly leave much to be desired. The abnormally high child mortality rate (particularly among blacks) in so wealthy a nation is especially disconcerting. Population-health metrics such as life expectancy at birth and child mortality, however, reflect a complex combination of population characteristics and social, economic, or cultural conditions, in addition to health systems characteristics. The latter obviously can have an impact on child mortality or life expectancy at birth by affecting care received by pregnant women and children or the prevention and treatment of disease in adults. However, other conditions beyond the purview of the health care system per se can also have a profound impact on child mortality or life expectancy. As a

TABLE 1-1

COMPARISON OF GENERAL POPULATION HEALTH METRICS,
UNITED STATES AND SELECTED DEVELOPED COUNTRIES, 2001

	Child Mortality (Age $\leq$ 5)[1]	Healthy Life Expectancy (Birth)[1]	Healthy Life Expectancy (Age 60)[1]
United States	9 (7)	66 (69)	15 (17)
White	7 (6)	67 (69)[2]	15 (17)[2]
Black	16 (13)	61 (65)[2]	14 (16)[2]
Australia	7 (5)	70 (73)	16 (19)
Canada	6 (5)	68 (71)	15 (18)
Denmark	6 (5)	69 (71)	16 (17)
France	5 (4)	69 (74)	16 (19)
Germany	5 (4)	68 (72)	15 (18)
Italy	6 (5)	69 (73)	16 (18)
Japan	5 (4)	71 (76)	17 (21)
Sweden	4 (3)	70 (73)	17 (19)
Switzerland	6 (5)	71 (74)	17 (20)
United Kingdom	7 (6)	68 (71)	15 (17)

SOURCES: World Health Organization (2004); U.S. Department of Health and Human Services (2004), race-specific data.
NOTES: 1. Male (female). 2. Imputed from ratio of total to race-specific life expectancy in years.

result, broad population-health metrics may not be sufficiently sensitive to differences in health-systems characteristics to serve as a meaningful measure of health-systems performance.

Definitional issues also can complicate cross-national comparisons of population-health metrics. For example, measures of child mortality can be sensitive to the definition of a live birth. A premature birth resulting in a nearly instantaneous death may be classified as a live birth and infant death in some countries (such as the United States), but as a fetal death in others. This definitional distinction affects measures of the oft-cited infant mortality rate, because a fetal death is absent from both the numerator and denominator of the infant mortality rate. An alternative health metric that (partially) avoids this definitional issue is perinatal mortality, where late fetal

TABLE 1-2

COMPARISON OF PERINATAL MORTALITY RATES,
UNITED STATES AND SELECTED DEVELOPED COUNTRIES, 2001

	Perinatal Mortality[1]
United States	7.2
White	6.2
Black	13.1
Canada	6.7
Germany	6.8
Japan	7.0
Sweden	6.5
United Kingdom	7.9

SOURCES: OECD (2003); U.S. Department of Health and Human Services (2004).
NOTE: 1. (Fetal Deaths + Neonatal Deaths)/[(Live Births + Fetal Deaths)/1000].

deaths are combined with early (neonatal) infant deaths. As shown in table 1-2, although the United States still underperforms relative to many other developed countries in perinatal mortality, the differences in the perinatal mortality rate here and in these other countries are considerably smaller than the differences in child mortality rates, at least for the overall population and among whites. However, the apparent underperformance remains pronounced among African Americans.

The abnormally high child mortality rate obviously contributes to the abnormally low life expectancy at birth in the United States. But death rates among adolescents and youth can also have a dramatic impact on estimated life expectancy. In that light, it is important to note that some specific cultural aspects of American society largely outside the purview of the health care system contribute to rates of death from injury, both unintentional (accidents) and intentional (homicide and suicide). Rates of death from injury are usually high in the United States compared to other developed countries, which affects the apparent underperformance of the U.S. health system (as measured by life expectancy at birth), because deaths from injury disproportionately affect adolescents and young adults.

TABLE 1-3
COMPARISON OF HEALTH OUTCOMES RELATIVELY INSENSITIVE
TO HEALTH CARE SYSTEM CHARACTERISTICS, 2000

	Homicide	Transport
United States	7.3	15.3
White	3.2	n/a
Black	26.1	n/a
Canada	1.4	9.3
Germany	0.9	10.1
Japan	0.6	8.3
Sweden	1.2	4.9
United Kingdom	0.7	6.0

SOURCES: World Health Organization (2004); U.S. Department of Health and Human Services (2002a).
NOTE: Death rate per 1,000.

According to data from the World Health Organization, the death rate from transport accidents (motor vehicle or common carrier) in the United States is about three times higher than the rate in Sweden or the United Kingdom, and one and a half to two times higher than in Australia, Canada, Denmark, Germany, or Japan (table 1-3). In the United States, unintentional injury was the fifth leading cause of death in the year 2000 overall, but was the leading cause of death among individuals between the ages of one and thirty-four, and was the second and third most common cause of death among individuals between the ages of thirty-five and forty-four and forty-five and fifty-four, respectively.[32] By contrast, among individuals sixty-five years of age and over, unintentional injury was the ninth leading cause of death. The unusually high death rates from unintentional injury among young Americans reduce the estimated life expectancy at birth for the United States, but they do not necessarily signal a deficiency in the U.S. health care system.

Although homicide is a much less common cause of death than unintentional injury in the United States, the difference between the U.S. homicide rate and that observed in other developed nations is nothing less than

Table 1-4

Estimated Relationship between Country-Level Life Expectancy at Birth and Fatal Unintentional and Intentional Injury Rates, OECD Countries, 1980–99

Variable	Parameter Estimate	Standard Error	p-value
Intercept	50.78	1.834	<0.01
Log (GDP per capita)	3.020	0.191	<0.01
Unintentional injury—Transport	−0.077	0.010	<0.01
Unintentional injury—Falls	0.137	0.013	<0.01
Intentional injury—Homicide	−0.133	0.013	<0.01
Intentional injury—Suicide	−0.033	0.011	<0.01
Year dummies	Included		
Adjusted R-squared	0.79		

Source: Estimated using OECD data, 1980–99.

astounding. According to WHO data, the U.S. rate is ten to twelve times greater than that of Japan or the United Kingdom, eight times greater than in France or Germany, and five to six times greater than in Australia, Canada, Denmark, Italy, or Sweden (table 1-3). This difference is even more dramatic if race-specific rates are examined. In 1998, among non-Hispanic whites, the homicide rate (per 100,000 population) was 3.2, as compared to 26.1 for non-Hispanic blacks and 9.9 for Hispanics.[33] Indeed, homicide was the *leading* cause of death among black males fifteen to thirty-four years of age in 2000.[34] Whatever societal ills contribute to the unusually high homicide rate in the United States, the health care system per se has little impact on it.[35]

Most deaths from unintentional or intentional injury (especially homicide) occur before the age of sixty. Thus, crossnational comparisons of healthy life expectancy at birth are related to differential death rates from injury, because estimates of life expectancy at birth are constructed from hypothetical cohorts based on contemporaneous mortality rates specific to age groups. To illustrate this point, we used OECD data for the years 1980

through 1999 to estimate a regression model relating crossnational variation in life expectancy at birth to variation in injury-death rates. The results
are reported in table 1-4. Obviously, a homicide involving a thirty-year-old
cannot literally affect the life expectancy of an infant, but it can affect estimates of life expectancy at birth constructed from contemporaneous mortality rates specific to age groups. Thus, the associations between the
injury-mortality rates and life expectancy at birth reflect the impact of
injury-death rates on age-specific mortality rates.

The regression estimates reported in table 1-4 can be used to produce
estimates of life expectancy at birth that have been "standardized" by the
mean injury-death rates across all OECD countries for the sample period.
Specifically, for each country (i) in each year (t), a predicted value for life
expectancy at birth is calculated:

EQUATION 1-1

$$\text{LifeExp}_{it} = 50.78 + 3.020 \cdot \log(\text{GDPPC}_{it}) - 0.077 \cdot [\text{mean(Trans)}]$$
$$- 0.137 \cdot [\text{mean(Falls)}] - 0.133 \cdot [\text{mean(Homicide)}]$$
$$- 0.0326 \cdot [\text{mean(Suicide)}] + \text{year-effects}_{it}$$

In equation 1-1, the term "mean(Trans)" refers to the mean transport injury-
death rate for all OECD countries over 1980–99, and likewise for the other
injury-death rates. The term "year-effects" indicates the presence of a binary
(dummy) variable in the regression model for each year in the sample and
its associated estimated coefficient (not reported).

The standardized estimate of life expectancy at birth is the mean of the
predicted value for each country over the period 1980–99. As shown in
table 1-5, the raw (not standardized) mean life expectancy at birth for the
United States over this period was 75.3 years, compared to 78.7 years for
Japan, 78.0 years for Iceland, and 77.7 years for Sweden. However, after
accounting for the unusually high fatal-injury rates in the United States, the
estimate of standardized life expectancy at birth is 76.9 years, which is
higher than the estimates for any other OECD country.

The differences in estimated standardized life expectancy among most
of the high-income developed countries in table 1-5 are small. Thus, this
exercise merely demonstrates that broad population-health metrics of this

TABLE 1-5

MEAN LIFE EXPECTANCY AT BIRTH, OECD COUNTRIES,
ACTUAL AND STANDARDIZED BY OECD MEAN FATAL INJURY RATES, 1980–99

	Actual Mean	Standardized Mean	Ratio (Std/Act)
United States	75.3	76.9	1.022
Switzerland	77.6	76.6	0.988
Norway	77.0	76.3	0.991
Canada	77.3	76.2	0.986
Denmark	75.1	76.1	1.014
Germany	75.4	76.1	1.009
Iceland	78.0	76.1	0.975
Sweden	77.7	76.1	0.979
Japan	78.7	76.0	0.967
Australia	76.8	76.0	0.990
France	76.6	76.0	0.992
Belgium	75.7	76.0	1.004
Austria	75.3	76.0	1.008
Netherlands	77.0	75.9	0.987
Italy	76.6	75.8	0.989
United Kingdom	75.6	75.7	1.002
Finland	75.4	75.7	1.005
New Zealand	75.4	75.4	1.000
Czech Republic	72.2	75.1	1.041
Ireland	74.8	75.0	1.002
Spain	77.3	74.9	0.969
Slovak Republic	71.6	74.4	1.040
Greece	77.1	74.4	0.964
Portugal	73.9	74.3	1.006
Hungary	69.7	74.3	1.066
Korea	71.1	73.3	1.030
Poland	71.5	73.2	1.023
Mexico	70.9	72.8	1.028
Turkey	64.4	72.0	1.118

SOURCE: Estimated from OECD data.

sort, after simple adjustments for outcomes essentially unrelated to health-systems characteristics, are not particularly sensitive to differences in health-systems characteristics.

In contrast to life expectancy at birth, cross-national comparisons of healthy life expectancy at age sixty are relatively unaffected by differential death rates from unintentional injury and homicide. Referring back to table 1-1, the apparent underperformance of the U.S. system is muted substantially, especially for African-American males, when healthy life expectancy at age sixty is used as a performance metric. Of course, part of the improvement may be due to the fact that the United States offers universal health care insurance for persons sixty-five years of age and over in the form of Medicare. To the extent that economic or racial disparities in access to care contribute to the low values of the usual population-health metrics in the United States, this impact would be less pronounced among those sixty-five and over.

When more specific performance metrics are used that are (at least potentially) more sensitive to health-systems differences, in many cases the United States does, indeed, appear to outperform other, less expensive health systems. Table 1-6 reports age-adjusted five-year survival rates for several types of cancers. In all cases, the survival rates for the United States overall exceed those for European nations. Within the United States, survival rates for whites are higher than those for African Americans. Presumably this, at least in part, reflects race differences in average socioeconomic status and access to health care. Even so, survival rates among African Americans tend to be on a par with the overall survival rates in European nations.

As always, it is important to exercise considerable care in making cross-national comparisons of specific health outcomes. Such comparisons could be seriously misleading due to differences in case definitions in other aspects of measurement across countries. For example, the cancer survival rate estimates reported in table 1-6 adjust for age at diagnosis but do not adjust for cancer stage at diagnosis. This could result in survivor time bias—those with cancers detected at an earlier stage would exhibit longer postdiagnosis survival times, even for cancers that are essentially untreatable.

Survivor time bias, however, should not be a significant concern for cancers that respond well to treatment if detected early. For such cancers, early detection makes a substantive contribution to survival time—the longer survival time associated with early detection thus is not a spurious

TABLE 1-6

FIVE-YEAR AGE-ADJUSTED CANCER SURVIVAL RATES,
UNITED STATES[1] AND SELECTED EUROPEAN COUNTRIES[2]

	Breast (Female)	Cervical (Female)	Colon (Male)	Lung (Male)	Prostate (Male)	Thyroid (Female)
United States	82.8	69.0	61.7	12.0	81.2	95.9
White	83.9	71.8	62.5	12.0	82.7	95.7
Black	69.2	55.6	52.6	12.0	69.2	93.0
England	66.7	62.6	41.0	7.0	44.3	74.4
Denmark	70.6	64.2	39.2	5.6	41.0	71.7
France	80.3	64.1	51.8	11.5	61.7	81.0
Germany	71.7	64.1	49.6	8.7	67.6	77.0
Italy	76.7	64.0	46.9	8.6	47.4	77.0
Sweden	80.6	68.0	51.8	8.8	64.7	83.7
Switzerland	79.6	67.2	52.3	10.3	71.4	78.0

NOTES: 1. U.S. National Cancer Institute (2003), year of diagnosis 1986–88. 2. International Agency for Research on Cancer (2003), year of diagnosis 1985–89.

effect of early detection. An example is thyroid cancer. In the United States, virtually all females with thyroid cancer survive for at least five years. The lower survival rates for thyroid cancer in European countries suggest some underperformance in either early detection or postdiagnosis management in these countries. In contrast, the differences in survivor rates are less pronounced for cancers that are more difficult to treat, such as lung cancers.

Similar themes are observed in a recent study by the Commonwealth Fund International Working Group on Quality Indicators, which collected data on twenty-one health care quality indicators from Australia, Canada, New Zealand, England, and the United States.[36] The measures included survival rates for nine different diseases and conditions (such as breast cancer and ischemic stroke), eight different avoidable events (such as suicide and hepatitis B), and four process indicators (such as breast cancer screening rate and influenza vaccination rate for individuals sixty-five years of age and over). Efforts were made to ensure reasonable comparability across countries. Among the five countries, the United States ranked either best or second-best in just over half of the twenty-one categories. It was first or second in three of the nine survival indicators (breast cancer, cervical cancer, and leukemia in children ages zero to fifteen), all but one of the eight avoidable-event indicators, and one of the four process indicators (cervical cancer screening rate). The authors conclude that "no country scores consistently the best or worst overall, and each country has at least one area where it could learn from international experience. Each country also has an area where it could teach others."[37]

Differences in population characteristics across countries also contribute to apparent differences in health system performance. Among them are patterns of health behavior, or "lifestyle." Traditionally, the United States has been by far the fattest developed country in the world, though rates of obesity have been increasing dramatically over the past two decades in several high-income developed countries.[38] In 2003, according to OECD data, the U.S. population still was the fattest, with 31 percent of the adult population being clinically obese—defined as having body-mass index (BMI) greater than 30.[39] This compares to an obesity rate of 23 percent in the United Kingdom, 9.4 percent in France, and 3.2 percent in Japan and Korea. There is abundant evidence that obesity contributes to premature death and increases U.S. health care costs. McGinnis and Foege conclude that in the United States obesity is second only to smoking as a contributor to premature death.[40] Sturm finds that total health spending among the obese (BMI > 30) is 36 percent higher—and pharmaceutical spending 77 percent higher—than among those not obese or overweight (BMI ≤ 25).[41] In a regression model using OECD and WHO data, Miller and Frech estimate that a 10 percent decrease in population-level obesity level (for example, from the then-OECD mean of 10 percent to 9 percent) increases disability-adjusted life-expectancy at age sixty by about 0.5 percent (or about thirty days).[42]

Other commonly cited lifestyle factors affecting health include tobacco and alcohol use. These indicators are not as unfavorable for the United States as obesity. In 2003, according to OECD data, the United States, Canada, and Sweden had the lowest rates of tobacco use among all OECD countries, and the United States ranked eleventh in alcohol consumption. Somewhat surprisingly, however, Miller and Frech found that population-level rates of tobacco and alcohol use were not statistically associated with life expectancy after adjusting for per-capita GDP and health spending.[43]

Finally, given the surge in obesity in several high-income countries over the last twenty years, coupled with a lag between the onset of obesity and its impact on premature death, one might expect the divergence in life expectancy at birth and other population-health outcome measures for the United States and other developed countries to diminish in the future.

Access to Care

Critics are unanimous in citing the lack of universal access to health care services or insurance coverage as one of the principal shortcomings of the U.S. health system, relative to health systems in other high-income developed countries. Lack of universal access generally is believed to be the most significant contributor to the underperformance of the U.S. system in terms of population-health measures.

The uninsured in the United States have a surprising degree of access to some types of care.[44] Asch and colleagues concluded that, among those who had at least one visit to a health care provider in the prior year, there were no differences across four process measures of quality of care between the uninsured and insured.[45] Nonetheless, many studies have found that those without health insurance tend to use fewer and different types of health care services than those with insurance, especially for preventive care. Delays in seeking care or a lack of a usual source of care among the uninsured can be associated with lower-quality care.[46] According to Schoen and colleagues, the underinsured experience health access problems remarkably similar to those of the uninsured, including failure to fill prescriptions, forgoing tests and treatment, and forgoing visits to regular doctors and specialists.[47] Rising premiums also can result in a larger number of uninsured as people drop coverage altogether.[48]

Researchers have devoted considerable effort to analyzing various aspects of the uninsured in America. According to the Census Bureau, there were about 46 million Americans without health insurance in 2004.[49] However, such estimates vary depending on who is counting, when, and what data are used.[50] Census estimates based on Current Population Survey (CPS) data are the most commonly cited. Although they indicate the number of uninsured has tended to trend upward over time, the percentage of the

FIGURE 1-5

UNINSURED POPULATION UNDER AGE 65, 1987–2004

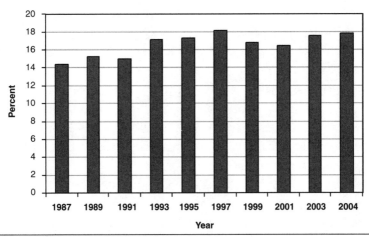

SOURCE: U.S. Bureau of the Census (2005b).

population under age sixty-five without health insurance does not exhibit any readily recognized trend, as shown in figure 1-5. What is most remarkable about the percentage of the population under age sixty-five who are uninsured in the United States is that it seems to be largely unrelated over time to variations in the business cycle and general macroeconomic conditions.[51]

Who are the uninsured, and why are they uninsured? Many are chronically uninsured, meaning they have had no health insurance over a multiyear period. Many of those who report in cross-sectional surveys that they are uninsured are not chronically uninsured but are in a transitional spell without insurance. Most of these transitional spells result from loss of benefits after a change in jobs or loss of Medicaid eligibility due to changes in household income; the median duration of these spells is less than twelve months.[52] Data concerning the duration of spells without insurance yield "half-empty versus half-full" interpretations. On the one hand, the cross-sectional measure significantly overstates the number of chronically uninsured individuals. On the other, the usual cross-sectional measure understates the number of individuals with "unstable" insurance coverage over time. Moreover, some of the insured have very limited coverage.[53]

Individuals who lose health insurance due to job change have the option to purchase an extension to bridge the spell under the Consolidated Omnibus Budget Reconciliation Act (COBRA) and the Health Insurance Portability and Accountability Act (HIPAA). But the purchase of optional extensions is rare, in part because individuals have to pay the full premium for an extension of the plan they had while employed—including the portion of the premium previously paid by their employer.[54] They cannot switch to a cheaper policy in response to the higher out-of-pocket premium. Many states have attempted to reduce spells without insurance for means-tested public insurance programs (such as Medicaid) by defining a minimum eligibility duration of twelve months or more, but the cost impact for state governments often is substantial.[55]

As shown in figure 1-6, the uninsured are disproportionately young adults between the ages of eighteen and thirty-four. Most are self-employed, have jobs in companies with only a few employees, or work only part-time. Some have existing health conditions that would preclude them from obtaining insurance in the individual market, but most in this age group are in good health and should be able to secure private insurance at some premium. Although any objective definition of the "ability to pay" for health insurance is problematic, about half of all adults without insurance are in households whose income exceeds the federal poverty level by 200 percent or more, and about 20 percent are in households whose income exceeds the poverty level by 400 percent or more.[56]

The reason most often given in surveys for not purchasing health insurance is that it is "too expensive."[57] But the meaning of this response is unclear; individuals who are young or perceive themselves to be at low risk may view insurance at prevailing premiums as a poor value, even if they have the financial means to pay. In this sense, some of the uninsured "choose" to be uninsured.[58] State regulations that require insurers to cover numerous types of services may exacerbate the problem. As will be discussed in more detail in chapter 4, these regulations, in effect, prohibit low-cost "bare-bones" or catastrophic health insurance policies.[59] But even when regulations permit bare-bones policies, traditionally they have not fared well in individual or small-group markets. This is beginning to change, as insurers are more actively marketing new low-cost policies with benefits designed to address the perceptions of low value among the healthy uninsured.[60]

FIGURE 1-6

UNINSURED POPULATION BY AGE, 1987–2004

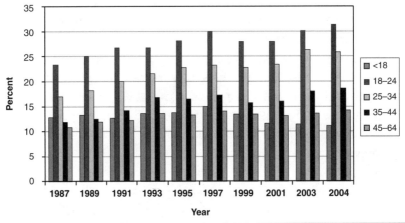

SOURCE: U.S. Bureau of the Census (2005b).

One clear trend in recent years has been a reduction in the percentage of children under age eighteen without health insurance (figure 1-6), primarily due to expansions in Medicaid coverage for children in low-income households. Another component of the uninsured population, however, consists of individuals who are eligible but not enrolled in Medicaid.[61] Such individuals may not be aware that they are eligible for Medicaid (especially those covered by recent expansions), or they may choose not to enroll, due to social stigma or other factors.

Finally, some of the people reporting in surveys that they have no health insurance do, in fact, have insurance. An estimated 10–20 percent of those counted as uninsured in the Census Bureau's analysis of CPS data had some form of insurance.[62] Many of these individuals were covered by Medicaid— they either forgot that they were covered or preferred not to report Medicaid coverage when responding to the survey. For instance, Klerman and colleagues found that Medi-Cal coverage was not reported in CPS for about 30 percent of recipients.[63] According to the Congressional Research Service, the most commonly cited estimates of the number of uninsured derived from CPS data reflect an undercount of individuals with Medicaid coverage of at least 10 million.[64]

Whether the number of uninsured in the United States is 30 million or 45 million, or whether the cause of uninsurance is a lack of information about eligibility or a lack of affordable private insurance among those with sufficient means to purchase it, there is near-unanimous agreement that the problem of the uninsured is the most significant shortcoming of the U.S. health system. There is no consensus, however, regarding the most appropriate solution for the problem, in part because the heterogeneous characteristics of the uninsured imply no simple "one size fits all" policy reforms.

In contrast to the United States, the impact of lack of insurance on access to care is largely a moot issue in other developed countries due to the presence of some form of universal health care or health insurance coverage. Individuals in these countries cannot be denied coverage or choose to be uninsured. However, access to health care services in these systems is limited by the availability of physicians, equipment, supplies, and spending caps, as well as policies concerning necessary or appropriate care. Few make use of financial incentives to control use, such as individual deductibles or coinsurance. The lack of price-rationing and the often limited availability of specialized personnel or equipment result in ubiquitous queues for many types of services in many systems, some of which are exceptionally long, at least by U.S. norms. For example, the mean waiting time for a magnetic resonance imaging (MRI) of the head in Canada in 1997 was one hundred fifty days, compared to three days in the United States.[65] Schoen and colleagues report that among sicker adults, 8 percent had to wait four months or more for nonemergency surgery in the United States, compared to 33 percent in Canada and 41 percent in the United Kingdom. Similarly, in the United States, 23 percent had to wait more than four weeks for an appointment with a specialist, compared to 57 percent in Canada and 60 percent in the United Kingdom.[66] Blendon and colleagues report similar findings for hospitalizations for elective surgery in the same five countries. The percentage of survey respondents reporting waiting times of four months or more for elective surgery ranged from 23 percent (Australia) to 38 percent (United Kingdom), compared to only 5 percent in the United States.[67]

Mechanisms for managing queues vary across health systems and by type of service. In some cases, no explicit criteria are used to prioritize individual patients in the queue, while in others, clinical criteria are used in an attempt to place those with a more immediate need for service closer to the front of the queue.[68] The latter approach often is hampered by a lack of consensus among experts concerning specific clinical criteria for prioritization,[69] but even in the absence of explicit criteria, in practice those patients with at least some characteristics suggestive of more proximate need tend to be assigned higher priority.[70] Nonetheless, an individual's placement in the queue is also to a degree influenced by nonclinical factors, such as nonclinical patient characteristics, characteristics of the referring physician or facility, or geographic location.[71]

Although deaths attributable to delays in treatment are rare, studies report high levels of anxiety among patients about perceived mortality risk during long delays.[72] For many, delays in treatment also delay the alleviation of symptoms, such as angina, osteoarthritis pain, or impaired vision. One study of patients' willingness to pay to reduce waiting time for cataract surgery to less than a month reported estimates of $128 in Canada, $160 in Denmark, and $243 in Spain (all in 1992 U.S. dollars).[73] In many of these countries, individuals with the means to do so can bypass queues by purchasing services from private providers (sometimes located in different countries).

A few countries explicitly prohibit the private provision of health care services. One used to be Canada, where private provision of services offered by the publicly funded Canadian health system (called Medicare) was not permitted. However, a recent decision of the Supreme Court of Canada overruled this prohibition. The majority opinion concluded that "access to a waiting list is not access to health care."[74] The majority opinion also noted the "unchallenged evidence that in some serious cases, patients can die as a result of waiting lists for public health care." The minority opinion countered that long waiting times were essential to help ration scarce resources, given that funds are limited while the demand for health care is not.

Providing "equally limited access for all" (instead of highly unequal access as in the United States) generally is presumed to be a key contributor to the superior population-health measures for non-U.S. health systems. Americans with health insurance who are accustomed to relatively unfettered access to care undoubtedly would chafe at the kinds of access restrictions that are routine in many other developed nations. Yet expanding the same sort of unfettered access to care currently enjoyed by the well-insured to the uninsured, with access unrestricted by queues or by price, almost certainly is not feasible, at least not at an acceptable cost.

Concluding Remarks

There is something of a consensus that improving access to care for the currently uninsured is a critical area for reform in the U.S. system. But there is no consensus about how to improve access; proposed solutions span the spectrum of administrative controls versus market incentives, from a single-payer government insurance system to mandated employer health benefits to consumer-directed, defined-contribution health spending accounts.

As noted, proponents of sweeping reforms often point to health systems in other developed nations as models to be emulated. However, as argued in this chapter, comparison countries have many shortcomings, and it is not at all clear whether the benefits of centralized control would offset the costs of a centralized system, were it to be implemented in the United States. Most health systems in other developed nations face unsustainable growth in spending and, in some cases, increasingly intolerable lapses in functional access. The same dynamic forces of population demographics and technological advances apply in these systems as well.

For health care consumers in the United States who have coverage, insurance provides a shield from the costs of the services they demand. This limited cost-sharing often results in excessive utilization of services. But even this limited cost-sharing is much greater than in the health systems of other developed nations, which typically entail little or no cost-sharing. As a result, global budget caps or other means of rationing access traditionally have been used. Indeed, health system reforms in these countries often entail decentralization of budgeting authority, or increasing reliance on patient cost-sharing, or incentive-based contracting with providers as a means of controlling expenditure growth.

Some effective means of addressing moral hazard is an essential element of any U.S. health system reform intending to create something close to universal health insurance coverage. There really are only two ways to accomplish this goal. One is effectively to limit access to care through administrative means, and the other is to use price incentives to discourage use of unnecessary care. We suggest that the latter approach is more compatible with prevailing preferences in the United States, and ultimately more likely to be successful as well.

2

Is Profit-Seeking Inappropriate in Health Care?

The most pernicious doctrine in health services research, the greatest impediment to clear thought and successful action, is that health care is different.

—James C. Robinson[1]

The belief that health care is *different* and therefore is (or should be) immune to factors that commonly affect the production or consumption of "mere commodities in exchange" has a long tradition and is deeply engrained among many health services and health policy researchers.[2] This self-evident "differentness" translates into a number of specific hypotheses about the unique consequences of market forces in the health care setting— market forces such as competition, entrepreneurialism, and price-rationing. In general, the differentness belief holds that, while such market forces might indeed work to improve consumer welfare in markets for some types of products, such as personal computers or household appliances, these same market forces often will harm consumers of health care. Thus, given the differentness of health care, the null hypothesis is that competition among health service providers degrades quality and increases costs, that profit-seeking entrepreneurs enhance profits by foisting inferior services on consumers, and that price-rationing is ineffective in allocating goods and services to those who value use the most.

The differentness belief is founded on two basic observations about health care. The first is that health care is essential to life. This is true enough, though it would be more accurate to state that in some circumstances health care can be essential. For example, health care is indeed essential for some types of acute conditions, such as trauma care following a serious injury. And, over time, health care for more chronic conditions can significantly extend or improve life. But much of what is termed health care is not "essential," in the sense that consumption (or lack of it) will have little or no permanent impact on health over the short term.

Even if most health care consumption is considered essential, as Robinson notes, food and shelter are even more essential to life, yet one does not observe policymakers fretting over the adverse impact of an excess capacity of grocery stores, or the potential for profit-seeking homebuilders to produce housing of inferior quality.[3] Or, rather, it probably would be accurate to observe that the degree of concern expressed generally is less pronounced, and focused on different alleged adverse effects. For example, policymakers often do fret about entry by a "super" Wal-Mart crushing small local grocery retailers, but the concerns generally relate to community aesthetics—even the harshest critics acknowledge that one result of such entry would be lower prices for consumers.[4] Clearly, essentiality cannot in and of itself support the differentness of health care.

Instead, the differentness belief rests on the combination of the essentiality assumption with a second and more salient observation about health care—that it is a complex good with a value that often is unknown to the consumer.[5] In general, whether or not a particular treatment, such as a surgical procedure or the use of a particular drug, will be beneficial to a particular individual depends on a number of factors. These include the clinical features of the consumer, the appropriateness of the surgical service or product as a treatment for the clinical condition, the quality of treatment, and the extent of risk associated with variance in treatment outcomes (cure versus serious adverse effects) when treatment is performed appropriately. All of these factors make it difficult for the consumer to assess the value of the treatment. The health care professional presumably is in a better position to assess the value of treatment than the potential patient. The concern is that providers of health care services might exploit this "informational asymmetry" between themselves and patients for personal gain, to the detriment of patients.

In a now-classic paper, Kenneth Arrow posited that some specific features of the health care sector might be attributable to asymmetric information between consumers and producers of health care services.[6]

Profit-seeking producers of services could enhance profits by exploiting the relative ignorance of consumers (presuming this tendency to exploit ignorance could remain undetected by the consumer). Thus, consumers might be less concerned about exploitation when obtaining services from not-for-profit producers (presuming not-for-profit producers are less focused on earning profits than for-profit producers). Likewise, professional ethics forbidding specific types of practice activities could serve to moderate any tendency among physicians and other health care professionals to exploit patient ignorance for personal gain.

But this begs the question: If consumers would be more likely to trust not-for-profit producers not to exploit their ignorance, why would the hospital-services sector have been dominated by not-for-profit organizations, while most nursing homes and virtually all physician practices were for-profit (or "for-net-income")? An equally plausible explanation for traditional dominance of not-for-profit hospitals is based on the historical development of hospitals. At the time hospitals bearing any resemblance to modern hospitals began to appear, most operated as not-for-profit organizations for a very simple reason—few people using hospital services were able to pay for them.[7] Those with financial resources or able family members typically were cared for at home, even when severely ill.

However, as medical science progressed, some types of useful services could be produced in hospitals more effectively than at home. Those who were able to pay were now also willing to pay for hospital care. Thus, it began to become possible to make a profit producing hospital care. The potential for profit in producing hospital services continued to grow with the expansion of employer-sponsored health insurance during and after World War II. In 1946, the federal Hospital Survey and Construction Act, better know as the Hill-Burton Act, funded a nationwide hospital-building program "to assist the several States in the carrying out of their programs for the construction and modernization of such public or other nonprofit community hospitals and other medical facilities as may be necessary, in conjunction with existing facilities, to furnish adequate hospital, clinic, or similar services to all their people."[8]

As new hospitals developed in the postwar period, they tended to operate as tax-exempt organizations, perhaps because of the not-for-profit hospital tradition, or because of the availability of Hill-Burton funds; or perhaps because physicians found not-for-profit hospitals to be more compliant with their wishes for resource availability,[9] or simply because some states prohibited entry by for-profit hospitals.

For-profit hospitals began to become more common after the implementation of Medicare and Medicaid programs, which provided (then) relatively generous government payment for hospital services consumed by the elderly (Medicare) and the very poor (Medicaid). Since many of the elderly and poor were previously uninsured, these programs substantially reduced exposure to potential uncompensated care, thereby reducing financial risk for for-profit entrants. Not surprisingly, for the most part, for-profit hospitals entered markets in states experiencing high rates of population growth, where state-level regulations did not present insurmountable barriers to entry.

The trust argument for tax-exempt hospitals is based on the assumption that they are less likely to exploit consumers to enhance profits. However, current evidence calls into question whether there is a "dime's worth" of difference in cost efficiency or quality of care between tax-exempt and for-profit hospitals.[10] Mergers between tax-exempt hospitals produce the same types of postmerger effects as those between for-profit hospitals.[11]

There is some evidence that for-profit hospitals are somewhat more aggressive in pursuing new profit opportunities than tax-exempt hospitals.[12] Mobley and Bradford argue that some of these apparent differences are attributable to the endogeneity of ownership form for entry and location choice.[13] But even if tax-exempt hospitals are less aggressive in pursuing potentially profitable ventures, the practical meaning of this finding is ambiguous—does it mean that for-profit hospitals are too entrepreneurial, or does it simply reflect managerial lethargy within tax-exempt hospitals?

In recent years, the fundamental basis for the tax-exempt status of not-for-profit hospitals has been questioned.[14] What social needs do not-for-profit hospitals fulfill to warrant their tax-exempt status? The most obvious answer is the provision of care to the uninsured or those otherwise unable to pay. Many private not-for-profit hospitals do, indeed, provide substantial charity care and must rely on significant contributions from donors to remain financially solvent. However, many other tax-exempt hospitals provide minimal charity care. In aggregate, the level of charity care provided by tax-exempt hospitals is approximately equal to the tax payments

FIGURE 2-1

TRENDS IN UNINSURED POPULATION AND
HOSPITAL UNCOMPENSATED CARE, 1991–2003

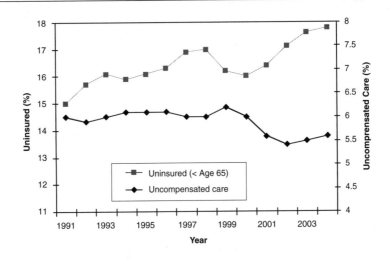

SOURCE: Adapted from Weissman (2005).

they avoid by virtue of their tax-exempt status.[15] Moreover, tax-exempt hospitals have been sued for charging higher prices to uninsured individuals who lack the pre-negotiated discounts common in contracts with commercial insurance payers.[16] Finally, the extent of charity care provision clearly is not strongly correlated with the size of the uninsured population, as illustrated in figure 2-1.

Impact of Competition

Another implication of the differentness belief is that competition in health care often will result in adverse effects for health care consumers, both in terms of increasing costs and degrading quality. The notion that competition among hospitals increases costs usually is based on some variant of the "medical arms race" hypothesis.[17] Under this hypothesis, hospitals competed by continuously acquiring the latest new technology (CT scanners and MRIs were common examples) or expanding service offerings. This would help the hospital to project an image of higher quality than its competitor. Unfortunately, the competitor would also acquire the new technology, setting in motion a vicious cycle of new and costly capacity expansions among competing hospitals.

The medical arms race, to the extent it occurred following the implementation of Medicare, was most directly a consequence of the original Medicare payment method for hospital services, based on reimbursement for hospital costs, coupled with an increasing prevalence of private hospital insurance with fee-based payment. The impact of the correspondingly limited price sensitivity among buyers was exacerbated by the tax-exempt status of hospitals, also predominant at the time, which required hospital profits to be reinvested (for example, in new ventures). Nonetheless, the solution policymakers selected to address this perceived problem was certificate-of-need (CON) programs. CON refers to a process through which a state regulates overall hospital capacity and offerings of specific hospital services within the state. Hospitals hoping to enter a market or offer a new service must demonstrate a justifiable need for the new capacity, to the satisfaction of the regulators, before being allowed to proceed.

The federal Health Planning Act of 1974, through a combination of incentives and penalties, for all intents and purposes required states to adopt CON programs. Federal funding for state health planning agencies was eliminated in 1982, and the federal health planning law itself was repealed in 1986 after Medicare cost-based payment was eliminated in favor of the current prospective payment system. Several states, primarily those experiencing high rates of population growth, repealed their CON programs in the 1980s, but they remain in effect in a majority of states.

There have been numerous studies of the impact of CON over the last three decades, focused on early adopters,[18] long-term effects,[19] and the impact of CON repeal.[20] In a recent review of the literature on CON, Conover and Sloan conclude that, "unlike many areas of research in health policy, research into CON effects on acute care costs provides a rather clear answer. CON has not succeeded in cost containment."[21] Indeed, the bulk of the literature indicates that CON increases costs.[22] In a similar vein, according to a recent study of health care markets by the Federal Trade Commission and the Department of Justice, "On balance, CON programs are not successful in containing costs, and . . . they pose serious anticompetitive risks that usually outweigh their purported economic benefits."[23]

Given its ineffectiveness at controlling health care costs, a more recent rationale for CON is that it may improve quality for some specific types of services by concentrating service provision in a limited number of facilities, thereby increasing the number of patients treated at high-volume facilities. This hypothesis is based on evidence that hospitals with higher volumes of specific services have outcomes superior to low-volume hospitals.[24] Indeed, a recent study found an association between CON and better outcomes for coronary artery bypass graft (CABG) surgery.[25] If CON can indeed improve quality for specialized services, would that justify using it to limit entry? Probably not. Just as CON was an extremely indirect and ultimately ineffective mechanism to address the underlying causes for the medical arms race, it is an unacceptably blunt instrument for quality enhancement in a sector as innovative and dynamic as health care.

A fundamental problem with CON is that it awards a property right—a monopoly franchise—to the recipient, often in perpetuity. The resulting rent-seeking behavior on the part of incumbents is as predictable as it is pervasive.[26] CON ossifies market structure and stifles innovation. If the state concludes that a regulatory limit on the number of hospitals offering cardiac surgery or other specific services is needed to assure an ongoing volume of services sufficient to maintain quality, a system of contestable franchises would at least be an improvement over CON. Another superior alternative would be periodic licensure (and relicensure) of these special-service units based on volume and other quality assurance considerations.

However, such regulation may not be needed at all. California is one of several states that repealed CON regulation after federal funding of state health planning activities was eliminated early in the Reagan administration. A recent study tracked entry and exit for CABG providers in California over the period 1984–94.[27] At the beginning of this period, the principal factor driving entry was a healthy return on investment resulting from generous payment from Medicare and other payers (with the exception of Health Maintenance Organizations [HMOs] and Medicaid). By the end of the period, declining Medicare payments and increasing price competition for contracts with other payers caused the return on investment to decline substantially.

Payers also have made note of the relationship between volume and outcomes. The Leapfrog Group for Patient Safety, founded by the Business Roundtable with support from the Robert Wood Johnson Foundation, has developed a set of guidelines for large employers as purchasers of health care services.[28] Among other things, these guidelines encourage payers to develop selective contracts for specific procedures with hospitals that produce a sufficient volume of the procedure to ensure adequate quality. The use of selective contracting to channel patients to high-volume procedures, if pervasive, would provide a powerful disincentive for entry by providers unlikely to attain target procedure volumes.

Both the robust price competition observed in California and the quality competition envisioned by the Leapfrog Group rely on the ability of payers to engage in selective contracting with providers. However, at least thirteen states have enacted "any willing provider" laws for hospitals.[29] These laws prohibit selective contracting for some types of insurers, and thus, at least in theory, limit the ability of payers to negotiate lower prices or exclude "low-quality" providers from provider panels. Recently, in *Kentucky Association of Health Plans v. Miller*, the U.S. Supreme Court rejected an attempt by payers to use the Employee Retirement Income Security Act (ERISA) to challenge the laws.[30] This decision may encourage more states to enact such laws.

Profit-Seeking and Product Quality

There is an extensive literature on the relationship among internal property rights, ownership form, and internal incentives for efficiency.[31] In contrast to for-profit organizations, in tax-exempt (or governmental) organizations, the ownership of the "residuals" (that is, rents or profits) produced by the organization is poorly defined. This lack of clearly defined residual claimants, at least in theory, mutes the incentive to improve product quality, enhance productive efficiency, or take any other action to enhance long-term profitability.

To illustrate the difference, suppose a manager in an organization comes up with an idea to increase revenues or decrease costs. In a for-profit organization, the manager would, in most cases, be rewarded, either with a substantial bonus or through appreciation in the value of his or her holdings of company stock. The same incentive would not be present for a manager in a tax-exempt organization, because tax-exempt organizations are precluded from distributing profits to owners according to their share of investment (because they lack ownership shares), and because they also are limited in their ability to distribute profit-sharing bonuses to employees. Similarly, a manager in a governmental organization who found a way to reduce costs, thereby producing a budget surplus, in all likelihood would be "rewarded" by having his or her departmental budget allocation reduced in the next budget cycle.

The theoretical implications of property rights within organizations of different ownership forms have been evaluated empirically across a wide array of industries.[32] Generally, these studies concluded that for-profit firms exhibit greater economic efficiency than not-for-profit or governmental organizations in many industries and similar efficiency in others (such as hospital-service production). Likewise, for-profit firms tend to be more innovative and focused on customer satisfaction in most industries, though less consistently so in the provision of health services. But the most important finding is that these differences in performance consistently are smaller in market areas where competition between for-profit and not-for-profit organizations is more pronounced.

There is substantial evidence that the quality of care generally improves with competition among hospitals. Looking at the impact of competition on costs and outcomes of hospital cardiac care, Kessler and McClellan conclude that "competition led both to substantially lower costs and significantly lower rates of adverse outcomes."[33] In a related study, the same authors found that a "higher market density of for-profit hospitals results in significantly lower hospital expenditures for [acute myocardial infarction] patients, with no consequential impact on their mortality or cardiac health."[34] Similarly, Kessler and Geppert found that competition improved the matching of resource utilization to patient acuity level, such that patients received levels of service that were more appropriate given the severity or complexity of their cases.[35] Specifically, patients with greater acuity received more resources and had better outcomes when treated in hospitals in competitive market areas relative to those treated in less competitive market areas. Patients with lower acuity in more competitive market areas received fewer resources but had outcomes similar to those treated in less competitive market areas.

Santerre and Vernon confirm that competition from for-profit hospitals induces greater productive efficiency in tax-exempt hospitals. As a result, "Too many not-for-profit and governmental hospitals may exist in the typical market area . . . [and] more quality of care per dollar might be obtained by attracting a greater percentage of for-profit hospitals into some market areas."[36] In a somewhat similar vein, Grabowski and Hirth conclude that competition from tax-exempt nursing homes induces quality improvement among for-profit nursing homes.[37] Thus, competition between for-profit and tax-exempt organizations may mitigate potentially adverse effects of either ownership form in isolation; the reduced temptation to exploit consumer ignorance among tax-exempt providers (because they have less to gain from doing so) may spill over onto for-profit providers, and the greater incentive for productive efficiency among for-profit firms may spill over onto tax-exempt firms. The essential point, however, is that in both cases the optimal mix includes at least some for-profit providers.

In many cases, however, the diminished managerial incentive to pursue profits in tax-exempt organizations may not result in a higher quality of care. A case in point is dialysis treatment for patients with end-stage renal disease (ESRD). A recent meta-analysis concludes that outcomes of treatment were systematically worse among for-profit as compared to tax-exempt dialysis centers. Indeed, the authors go so far as to conclude that 2,500 dialysis deaths could be avoided annually if all dialysis treatment were provided at tax-exempt centers.[38] The authors attribute the seemingly superior outcomes to higher resource utilization (and costs) at tax-exempt centers. Thus, the implication is that the quest for profits causes for-profit providers to "skimp" on resources needed to provide high-quality care, resulting in a higher mortality rate among those treated at for-profit centers.

An important limitation across the studies included in the meta-analysis is that they assumed any differences in the pattern of patients treated across dialysis centers of different ownership types could be accounted for using a few patient characteristics for risk-adjustment across treatment sites. This approach requires an assumption that any other factors that might affect outcomes are the same across sites. However, due to historical patterns of development and differences in state-level regulation, the prevalence of tax-exempt and for-profit dialysis centers varies considerably across states— states with very different population characteristics and ESRD death rates.

Further, there is considerable variation in relative distance to for-profit or tax-exempt dialysis centers among patients. Brooks and colleagues use differential distance as an instrumental variable (IV) for the patient's choice of dialysis center. The basic concept is that patients who are otherwise similar (in terms of disease severity or other individual characteristics that may affect mortality risk) would tend to be more likely to use a for-profit center if it is relatively closer than a tax-exempt center, and vice versa. Thus, relative distance maps into "quasi-random" variation in use of different types of dialysis centers among clinically similar patients. Using this IV model, Brooks and colleagues find no differences in outcomes between for-profit and tax-exempt dialysis centers. They conclude that "lower resource use at for-profit dialysis centers did not jeopardize the survival of new elderly ESRD patients and policies designed to reduce the number of for-profit dialysis centers may increase costs without increasing patient survival."[39]

Market versus Nonmarket Organization: A Comment on Single-Payer Initiatives

In the previous chapter, the U.S. health care system was compared to the systems of other developed countries, many of which maintain some form of universal access to health care services. Comprehensive systems, such as government-administered, single-payer plans, have been largely kept off the table of feasible reform alternatives in the U.S.[40] In California—long the breeding ground for innovations in health care management and organization—a proposal to create a large-scale, comprehensive, single-payer government health system—much like those created in Canada and Great Britain—has surfaced in the form of Senate Bill 840 (SB 840). The California proposal promises to extend health care coverage to all California residents, administered and funded centrally through state government.

The foremost nominal objective of the proposal—to extend coverage to all[41]—is laudable, for many of the reasons discussed in chapter 1. However, all health care reform proposals are associated with tradeoffs—incentives versus access, innovation versus stability, and adaptation versus control. These tradeoffs are complex and interrelated. Moreover, given that the United States has yet to experience the full feasible set of state and national health reforms, much of the knowledge concerning how various reforms would work here is based on applications of theory from the disciplines of economics, political science, and organizational sociology, coupled with the experiences of countries that have systems resembling those envisioned in various reform proposals. For example, Japan's system is akin to employer mandates, and Canada and Great Britain rely on single-payer, government-run systems.

The California single-payer bill, referred to as the "California Health Insurance Reliability Act" (CHIRA), would establish the California Health Insurance System (CHIS), which would be administered by the newly created California Health Insurance Agency (CHIA) under the control of an elected commissioner.[42] The bill would make all California residents eligible for a generous range of services, including inpatient and outpatient services, durable medical equipment, hearing aids, rehab care, preventive care, home health care, prescription drugs, mental health care, and many others.[43] Providers of these services would negotiate with CHIS on acceptable fees and minimum quality standards.[44] Interestingly, the bill emphasizes that CHIS will use its monopsony buying power (that is, buying power associated with a sole purchaser) to negotiate lower prices with pharmaceutical companies, but does not use the same language when discussing physician and hospital-service procurement.[45]

A number of support agencies would also be created, including a health insurance policy board, an office of consumer advocacy, an office of health planning, and an office of health care quality. These organizations would share responsibilities for technology assessment, coverage decisions, capital allocations, and minimum quality thresholds. The office of health care quality would be led by a chief medical officer (CMO), who would be responsible for defining and identifying appropriate and necessary medical services, implementing evidence-based medicine and clinical practice guidelines, establishing formularies, and working closely with the Commissioner in monitoring virtually all aspects of provider operations.

The act would create up to ten "health planning regions" throughout the state. Regional planning directors would be responsible for working with CHIS to establish, for example, global operating budgets for physician groups and hospitals, capital budget targets for the region (including review of providers' proposed capital projects), and physician specialty mixes.

The plan would effectively eliminate the private health insurance industry in California: "No health care service plan contract or health insurance policy, except for the [CHIS] plan, may be sold in California for services provided by the system."[46] As of the July 2005 amendments, the act does not appear to make any provisions for the effects on the California economy of eliminating a $51.5 billion industry.

The total annual costs of CHIS are expected to be $166.8 billion.[47] Financing is based on two direct sources: continued funding of existing government programs for Californians, including federal, state, and local programs ($72.2 billion), and new, dedicated taxes ($94.6 billion). The bulk of the continued funding is Medicare and Medi-Cal ($54.9 billion). Newly created taxes will likely include an 8.2 percent employer payroll tax ($55.7 billion), a 3.8 percent employee payroll tax, a 12 percent self-employed business income tax ($8.3 billion), a 4 percent nonwage/nonbusiness tax ($3.5 billion), and a 1 percent surcharge on incomes over $200,000 ($1.3 billion). The justification for the new taxes is that there will be significant savings to employers and employees in the form of shifting health care costs to state government, as well as system-wide savings attributable to greater efficiency and reductions in administrative costs.[48]

As we emphasized earlier in this chapter, single-payer plans do not guarantee universal access and do not necessarily result in high-quality health care. But even if universal government systems did deliver better care, access and quality are not sufficient criteria for administrative feasibility, viability, and longevity. Single-payer systems must deal with many of the same problems common to the existing hybrid system, such as financing, adverse selection, moral hazard, opportunism and fraud, innovation, and adaptation.

One of the commonly reported virtues of single-payer plans is their supposed advantage in cost-control and efficiency. One part of the cost and efficiency attributes of single-payer plans is, at least in theory, the reduction of administrative costs. As the preceding discussion emphasized, this advantage is illusory. There are sure to be reductions in overall administrative costs, but those reductions will be small if the single-payer plan continues to provide a reasonable level of value-added organizational and patient-care management, including such activities as disease management, patient education, provider management, quality control, and fraud and abuse monitoring. In addition, there are likely to be reductions in duplicative services, although not nearly to the extent supporters generally believe. Canada, for example, has been shown to have less medical equipment per capita than the United States,[49] but the lower levels of duplication are more commonly attributed to the fact that the structure of the Canadian health care system was essentially frozen in its 1960s state—when the laws creating the national system were passed—rather than to the ongoing effects of the system on capacity control.[50]

There are no structural attributes of single-payer plans that can effectively mitigate the cost effects of technological advances, an aging population, growing demands for high-quality care, and moral hazard. Bulk purchasing is often touted as a cost-saver, but the savings are most likely exaggerated. In order for bulk purchasing to work, the state has to be willing to walk away from the table when a large pharmaceutical manufacturer refuses to lower the price of a patented drug. This poses a potentially volatile problem of having abruptly to withdraw popular drugs from the formulary, or cease coverage for other popular products, such as cardiovascular stents. Moreover, Canada is often cited as a successful example of bulk purchasing, but strict price controls and lower GDP per capita are likely to play a much more prominent role in cost control.

These factors, and others, have resulted in cost pressure in virtually all of the single-payer systems internationally, particularly Canada and the United Kingdom, causing the systems to undergo significant reform against a backdrop of considerable consumer and provider discontent.[51] For example, annualized growth rates in per-capita spending from 1970 to 2002 were 5.1 percent for the United States, but countries with universal coverage were close behind, with average annual rates of increase of 3.1 percent (Canada), 3.7 percent (United Kingdom), 4.1 percent (Australia), and 4.9 percent (Japan).[52] Canada's health care spending is expected to increase between 7 percent and 10 percent annually in the next several years.[53]

Another potential health expenditure issue is adverse selection. Adverse selection occurs when consumers at comparatively higher risk in terms of predicted health care costs ("high-risk" consumers) purchase or enroll in risk pools comprised of a mix of high-risk and low-risk enrollees. To the high-risk consumer, enrolling in a plan comprised of a mix of enrollees is attractive because the average premiums will normally be lower than if they were to purchase insurance individually. As this process recurs, predicted costs for the entire risk pool rise. This phenomenon is quite common in private health insurance markets, and is one of the main justifications for constraining the ability to enter and exit group insurance policies (by imposing limited "open enrollment" periods, for example).

The proposed CHIS is only partially protected from adverse selection. By compelling all Californians to enroll in the CHIS plan, the program will pool low-risk and high-risk patients. However, the legislation as it is currently written does not explicitly call for a mandatory waiting period for new-resident eligibility.[54] The Lewin simulation models assume that the commissioner will implement a three-month residency requirement as a condition of eligibility, but then further assume (correctly) that the commissioner will have to make an exception for those relocating to California for the purpose of employment.[55] Presumably, it would be impractical to define or discern "eligible employment" from other kinds of employment (for instance, part-time versus full-time); thus, the employment exception will essentially neuter the effects of a waiting period.

The California plan relies extensively on rate and capacity regulation, which throughout the economy has been shown to result in low efficiency and high costs. Schneider, for example, recently reported that hospitals located in all-payer, rate-regulated states in 1984 and 1991 had operating costs approximately three to four percentage points lower than their less-regulated counterparts.[56] By 1996, however, the effect of rate regulation on hospital costs was reduced to approximately −0.4 percent, a result that narrowly achieved statistical significance ($p \leq 0.10$). Hospitals in less competitive markets were more likely to have higher operating costs, an effect that increased in magnitude over time. The results imply that hospitals in markets with comparatively less rate regulation or more competition have lower operating costs than their regulated or less-competitive counterparts.

Capacity regulation, which appears to be a critical component of CHIRA,[57] has also been shown to have deleterious effects on efficiency. Studies of the impact of CON programs have consistently found them to be ineffective at controlling costs and enhancing access, and, in some cases, they have been shown to increase costs.[58] In sum, while protecting incumbent hospitals from competitive entry may help achieve planning goals, the same insulation from competition is likely to allow incumbent firms to maintain higher prices and higher costs.

The financing of single-payer plans typically relies on tax revenue, either from general collections or targeted taxes, as have been proposed under CHIRA. Growth in public systems is controlled by bureaucrats and politicians, rather than consumers and market forces. Conversely, in a private system, increases in demand for certain kinds of services and increases in consumers' "willingness to pay" for medical services (including new technologies and procedures) will be countered with a supply-side response to adapt to those changes in demand. Financing for the changes will typically be generated by the industry; if consumers want it, they will be willing to pay for it.

A public system must also find a way to adapt to changes in consumer demand, but the financing necessary for adaptation flows from a single state government source. There is no guarantee that bureaucrats and politicians will be able to finance the system at levels aligned with consumer demand, nor is there any guarantee that, in the aggregate, consumers will be willing to vote in favor of tax increases sufficient to fund adaptation and growth. Funding adjustments are a function simultaneously of

- voter preferences for higher or lower taxes,

- competing demands from other state-funded programs,

- weak political property rights (such as funding or defunding to garner votes in election years),

- competing demands from within the system (such as the commissioner wanting to cut costs while general practitioners want to increase funds), and

- changes in medical practice patterns and consumer demand.

Residents of countries in which single-payer plans are available consistently indicate that the single most important action government can take to improve the system is "spend more money."[59] Budget cutbacks in Canada in the mid- to late-1990s, for example, resulted in a precipitous drop in the proportion of Canadians describing their health system as excellent or very good.[60] According to Abelson and others, "Canadians' anxiety seems to have peaked when reductions in federal government health care contributions were most severe. Since then, federal government increased its contributions as part of its 2000 pre-election health care budget."[61]

A final comment on CHIS financing has to do with the public financing climate in California. It would be difficult to argue that K–12 primary education is of less value than health care. Nevertheless, California has systematically underfunded K–12 education, choosing instead to maintain unusually strict limits on growth in property taxes. Since the passage in 1978 of Proposition 13, which limited property tax increases to a maximum of 2 percent per year, California's public school system has steadily degraded and currently ranks among one of the worst in the nation in terms of funding and performance.[62] Although there is no direct evidence to suggest that CHIS financing will be similarly constrained, it is reasonable at least to question whether CHIS financing will somehow be immune to the tenacious forces that passed and continue to uphold the current funding levels for public education in California.[63]

There are a number of ways in which to organize economic activity, the most prevalent examples of which include free markets, regulated markets, hierarchical organizations, and government organizations (that is, public administration or public governance). No form of organization is, per se, superior; each has its merits, and each is designed to facilitate specific kinds of transactions.[64] A critical component of the assessment of centralized government health care systems is to identify the comparative strengths and weaknesses of public versus private governance. Public governance seems to work well for defense, parks, police and safety, and the like. But apart from those familiar examples, there are many goods and services for which the public versus private question is largely unresolved. These include utilities, education, prisons, health care, transportation, and other traditionally governmental services, such as the armed services.[65]

For a given organizational problem or issue, such as extending health care to all, the pivotal question should be, "What does public administration have to offer?" The key differentiator, as Williamson has maintained, lies in the ability of these types of organizations to adapt to change.[66] An important omission from preliminary reports on the California single-payer proposal is a simulation of how private plans and government plans are likely to differ in their ability to adapt to changes in the health care marketplace. Bureaucracies are relatively good at adaptation that requires a coordinated response,[67] but the set of feasible responses within a bureaucracy are typically small in number, due in part to bureaucratic inertia and established routines.[68] Conversely, autonomous organizations are better at the kind of adaptation that requires timely responses to changes in demand, prices, and operating costs.

For example, coordinated government bureaucracies such as the U.S. Postal Service are relatively good (that is, efficient) at performing certain tasks, but they have clearly been followers in the delivery industry, as innovative and adaptive firms like Federal Express and United Parcel Service captured large market shares by out-innovating their government counterpart.[69] All else equal, gains from bureaucratic coordination, which the U.S. Postal Service does well, are often offset by incentive attenuation. This includes reduced incentives to attract new customers, invest in up-to-date capital and equipment, and innovate (processes and products), and reduced productivity from the reduced ability of decision-makers and risk-takers to share in entrepreneurial returns.

The health care system is dynamic and evolving. The evidence suggests that the vast majority of health care innovations have positive economic value, the total value of which exceeds the costs.[70] For example, the most expensive and, in many cases, valuable prescription drugs in the United States are newer drugs that are under patent.[71] A state health insurance system like CHIS is at risk of failing to innovate quickly enough to keep pace with the rapidly changing health care industry. Health care is a moving target; consumer preferences evolve and change as often as every year. How will a state-run program handle changes in consumer demand, in medical technology, and in input prices, such as wages? How will a state program handle geographic variations in charges? Will more concentrated provider groups command higher reimbursement rates? Will rural physicians be paid less than urban physicians? These are just a few examples of some potentially very difficult choices that could become intractable under the state-run system as the smallest of details requires legislative action.

Some more general characteristics of public administration are also of particular importance in the delivery of health care, and they add complexity to the aforementioned adaptation problems. One is the issue of "weak political property rights." Heclo observed that, in public administration, "would-be leaders among political executives are in a peculiarly weak political position in relation to each other and in relation to career bureaucrats."[72]

Similarly, Moe observed that "in politics, people with very different interests engage in a struggle to control and exercise public authority . . . because public authority does not belong to anyone—it is up for grabs—and because it is enormously valuable." He further asserted that the process produces winners and losers, and the winners can "promote their own interests through policies and structures of their own design [which] may entail very substantial costs for the losers, who have no choice but to accept what the winners dish out" and that "people can be forced to accept outcomes that make them worse off, outcomes they would never agree to in a world of voluntary exchange."[73]

The implications of these structural characteristics are far-reaching,[74] but in simple terms the problem with regard to CHIRA can be expressed as "politicized medicine" or "politicized health." The CHIS is structured much like any other government bureaucracy, governed externally by elected leaders (the legislature, the governor, and the commissioner) and internally by what Heclo describes as "career bureaucrats." Compared to the private health care system, the centralized system creates two new issues: elected leaders will govern the system so as to maximize political return (among their voting base), and internal bureaucrats will generally resist change in favor of the status quo.[75]

An additional and particularly troublesome feature of centrally planned health care governance is that, by design, elected leaders can win voter approval by using the system to further political agendas; for example, by excluding coverage for diseases and conditions that disproportionately affect gays, immigrants, drug users, and so on. A reporter for the *Ottawa Citizen* wrote, "For far too long Canada's health care system has been treated like a political football by Canada's politicians . . . the system has been used and abused for political attacks and political gains."[76]

Concluding Remarks

When Kenneth Arrow wrote his now-classic 1963 paper, the "Marcus Welby" model of medical practice was predominant. Physicians would issue orders; the patient's role was to comply with orders. But development of the information age has substantially attenuated the traditional informational asymmetry between physicians and patients. As Robinson notes, "Patients, consumers and citizens are ever more educated with respect to their own health and health care."[77] The development of the Internet has been especially important, as it gives patients the ability to "Google" a topic and download information about diseases from authoritative sources with minimal effort. Thus, some patients—particularly those with chronic diseases or rare conditions—will "have more, not less, information than their treating physicians."[78] The information explosion means that physicians, particularly primary care physicians, cannot know everything about every condition they treat. They often find themselves faced with a patient bringing in "a stack of articles downloaded from clinical journals that the doctor has no time to read."[79] Clearly, not all patients possess the means or initiative to acquire such information, or the capacity to translate what is learned into an appropriate treatment plan. "Obviously," writes Robinson, "the typical physician will always understand clinical medicine better than the typical patient; that is why we send young people to medical school."[80]

At least in principle, clinical practice has been making a transition from the paternalistic command-and-control model of old to a model of shared decision-making between patients and physicians, which in many ways is simply an extension of the concept of informed consent.[81] This movement in the conceptualization of the physician-patient relationship is consistent with the trends in information technology cited by Robinson,[82] though many physicians remain resistant[83] and at least some patients prefer a more passive role.[84] Nonetheless, even a minority of active and informed consumers can have a dramatic and disproportionate impact on the functioning of markets.

Clearly, health care is not a simple, virtually homogeneous commodity, such as a barrel of "West Texas Intermediate" crude oil, and simplistic market models that may be applicable to such simple commodities are for the most part not applicable to it. But many of the aspects of health care that make it seem unique are observed in other complex services and goods. A variety of institutions and organizational forms have evolved to enable markets for such products to function effectively, despite their complexity. Within the context of these institutions and organizational forms, however, the available evidence suggests that competition in health care spurs innovation, induces efficiency, and enhances quality, just as it does in other types of markets.

3

Competition in Hospital Markets:
The Case of Specialty Hospitals

In the previous chapter we discussed some of the ways in which market organization has generally worked well in health care markets, and how the suppression of market forces has generally resulted in higher costs and, at best, no appreciable increases in quality and outcomes. In this chapter we discuss an instance in which the benefits of competition are constrained by regulatory policy. Hospital specialization has become a controversial topic in recent years, culminating in a moratorium issued in 2003 by Congress directing the Centers for Medicare and Medicaid Services (CMS) to cease reimbursements to new physician-owned specialty hospitals for Medicare and Medicaid patients referred by physicians with a financial interest in the facility.[1] The moratorium, which was added to existing laws in many states prohibiting the operation of some types of specialty hospitals, was in part a response to the concern among incumbent general hospitals that specialized facilities might harm the community by undermining the ability of general hospitals to internally cross-subsidize unprofitable services, many of which might be considered essential to the community.[2]

This chapter focuses on two interesting and important economic questions raised by the moratorium. First, are there meaningful economic advantages associated with hospital specialization, such as lower costs or higher quality? If so, barriers to entry, such as the moratorium, could adversely affect consumer welfare. Second, does the presence of specialty hospitals in a market reduce the operating margins of general hospitals? If so, specialty hospitals may reduce consumer welfare by inhibiting the ability of general hospitals to cross-subsidize necessary but unprofitable services, such as emergency care and other services disproportionately provided to low-income groups.

This chapter has three sections. The first addresses the efficiency rationale for hospital specialization, providing a review of the theory and evidence regarding hospital economies of scale, economies of scope, learning, and core competencies. The primary sources of data are published literature, reports, a survey of specialty hospitals,[3] and site visits to specialty hospitals.[4] The second section reviews the literature on the effects of specialty hospitals on costs, case mix, volume, quality, and competition. It relies on many of the same sources as the first, but it also reports the results of a statistical analysis of the effects of specialty hospitals on general hospital operating margins. The final section discusses some of the important policy implications of these findings.

Hospital Specialization

During the latter half of the twentieth century, industries began exploring new ways to organize production. One of the most prominent of these changes was the adoption of lean production, flexible specialization, and focused factories, which resulted in many business establishments becoming less diverse and more focused.[5]

The hospital industry appears to be following a somewhat similar path with the growth of freestanding specialty hospitals and specialized units within general hospitals.[6] Specialty hospitals are typically defined as those that treat patients who have specific medical conditions or are in need of specific medical or surgical procedures.[7] The former specialize in psychiatric care, cancer care, rehabilitation, women's care, children's care, and certain chronic diseases; the latter specialize in cardiac, orthopedic, and general surgery. As of 2002, the total number of specialized hospitals (that is, all categories combined and including Medicare psychiatric and rehabilitation distinct-part units of general hospitals) was approximately 2,500 (table 3-1).

Recent political controversies surrounding specialty hospitals have focused primarily on facilities specializing in cardiac, orthopedic, and general surgery and, to a lesser extent, obstetrics and gynecology. There are

TABLE 3-1
TRENDS IN NUMBERS OF SPECIALTY HOSPITALS, 1995 AND 2002

Facility Type	1995	2002	Percent Change 1995–2002
Short-Term General Hospitals[a]	5,194	4,927	–5.4
Psychiatric[a, b, c]	1,402	1,436	2.4
Rehabilitation[a, b, c]	675	936	38.7
Cancer[b]	9	11	22.2
Obstetrics and Gynecology[d, e]	12	18	41.7
Orthopedic and General Surgery[d, e]	60	80	33.3
Cardiac Surgery[e, f]	10	17	70.0

NOTES: a. American Hospital Association (1997, 2004); b. Centers for Medicare and Medicaid Services (1995, 2002); c. Includes both freestanding hospitals and distinct units (as defined by CMS) within general hospitals; d. Based on authors' survey of ASHA members conducted in 2004; e. U.S. General Accounting Office (2003a); f. MedCath Corporation (2006).

approximately 100–120 of these hospitals currently operating in the United States. Growth in surgical hospitals ranged from 33 percent (orthopedic and general surgery) to 70 percent (cardiac surgery) during the seven-year period from 1995 to 2002. Most of these facilities are located in states without CON programs,[8] which regulate the construction and augmentation of health care facilities.[9] States with the highest concentrations of surgical specialty hospitals are South Dakota, Kansas, Oklahoma, Texas, Louisiana, Arizona, and California. The focus of controversy on surgical hospitals appears to be rooted in concerns over physician ownership and self-referral.[10] Approximately 70 percent of surgical hospitals have at least some level of physician ownership.[11]

Economic Rationale for Hospital Specialization

Recent reports on specialty hospitals suggest that the primary motivations for entry fall into three categories: consumer demand, administered pricing, and economic and clinical efficiency.[12] Demand for specialized inpatient and outpatient services has been growing rapidly in the past decade.[13] This is most likely due to a combination of factors, including increased incidence of specific diseases, new treatment processes and technologies, and changes in consumer preferences. Analogous to industries unrelated to health care, the hospital industry has been the subject of renewed emphasis on quality of care and customer satisfaction. In response, general and specialty hospitals alike have developed consumer-oriented centers of care focused on providing a limited range of services tailored to the specific needs of patients.[14]

An additional motivation for market entry is likely to be the existence of above-average profit margins on certain procedures. Prospective administered-pricing mechanisms create incentives for general and specialty hospitals alike to focus on diagnosis categories and procedures where the administered price exceeds average costs. Medicare's prospective pricing system (PPS) has been shown to affect the scope of services offered by acute-care hospitals. The PPS employs a fee schedule based on approximately five hundred diagnosis-related groups (DRGs); each is mapped to a price, with some hospital-specific adjustments. Payment by DRG provides strong incentives to hospitals to specialize in those for which they have relatively low production costs.[15] In the context of specialty hospitals, Robinson posits that "the success enjoyed by the specialized firms reflects astute selection of services and markets as much as efficiency in delivering care."[16] As is the case in any industry, we would expect to observe market entry into products and services for which operating margins are relatively high.

Specialty hospitals are likely to capture clinical and economic efficiencies. Clinical efficiencies include the ability of physicians to directly control quality of care, scheduling, the triaging of patients to the most appropriate settings, and equipment utilization and purchasing.[17] For example, Casalino, Pham, and Bazzoli report that one of the motivating factors for single-specialty medical groups was to "avoid the complicated governance and operational issues engendered by having primary care and specialty physicians in the same organization."[18] Economic efficiencies include economies of scale and scope in specialized procedures, learning-by-doing, and focus on core competencies.

Economies of scale exist if the average costs of producing a product or service decline as the volume of production increases. The evidence on economies of scale in the production of hospital services, while highly variable, indicates that U.S. general hospitals typically experience scale economies up to approximately ten thousand discharges per year.[19] However, the same evidence suggests that scale economies vary significantly by product and service line. In order to assess the potential role of scale economies in specialty hospital efficiency, scale economies for specific services (for example, total knee replacement) in specialty hospitals would need to be compared to those in general hospitals. While we are not aware of any study that does this, we do know that the volume of many specific surgical procedures performed at specialty hospitals typically exceeds that performed at general hospitals within the same market area.[20] Thus, to the extent economies of scale exist in these specific procedures, they are likely to be realized to a greater degree in specialty hospitals as compared to general hospitals.

In some cases, the joint production of two or more products or services can be accomplished for less than the combined costs of producing each individually. This is often the case when production relies on common resources, such as technology, workers, inputs, and general overhead. Such cases are said to exhibit economies of scope.[21] The decision to specialize will depend in part on the extent to which firms' existing scope of products and services exhibits diseconomies of scope (that is, where joint production is more costly than separate production). Conversely, the decision to diversify will in part be based on the extent to which joint production costs are less than separate production costs.

Evidence on economies of scope in the U.S. hospital industry is inconclusive. Menke found limited evidence of inpatient-outpatient scope economies in chain and nonchain hospitals.[22] Similarly, Fournier and Mitchell found significant scope economies among select outpatient services and surgery services, but their study was based on twenty-year-old data from one state.[23] Sinay and Campbell examined 262 merging acute-care hospitals in the United States during the period 1987–90.[24] Of the service pairings studied, evidence of economies of scope was found between acute care and subacute care (in merging hospitals) and between intensive care and outpatient visits (in control hospitals); all other pairings showed either diseconomies of scope (for instance, acute care and outpatient care, and intensive care and subacute care) or were statistically insignificant. Rozek failed to observe scope economies in general hospital diversification into psychiatric services, and Li and Rosenman's study of hospitals in the state of Washington was inconclusive.[25] As the lack of consistent findings on economies of scope suggests that they are not likely to be a significant source of production economies for general hospitals, it would be difficult to argue that specialty hospitals are less efficient than general hospitals due to their absence.

Skinner stressed that "simplicity, repetition, experience, and homogeneity of tasks breed competence."[26] Learning occurs as the experience of production in one time period influences the production in a later period; that is, the production process is assumed to have some degree of flexibility and can change over the relevant range of output.[27] The implication is that the costs of producing the first batch of output are greater than those of producing a subsequent batch due to the learning that occurred during the production of the first batch. Assuming that experiences of producing the first batch can be applied to the second (and other subsequent batches), the average costs of production are expected to decline as output cumulates over time. The learning effect will depend on the ability of the firm to process information during the production process and then apply that information appropriately.

The learning process is critical to the formation and adaptation of organizational routines, which include rules of thumb, guidelines, templates, and protocols.[28] Specialized routines are the subcomponents of organizational "know-how" and "core competencies," and are often sources of comparative advantage and production economies.[29] Core competencies refer to firms' existing stock of knowledge assets (including tacit knowledge and know-how), skills, and resources. By diversifying and expanding into activities that are related to core competencies, firms are typically able to take better advantage of the learning process and improve managerial efficiency.[30] In addition, limiting expansion into related business lines is likely to minimize some of the negative tradeoffs associated with growth in firm size, such as influence costs and other forms of incentive attenuation.[31] Consistent with Skinner's emphasis on the value of repetition, concentrating on core competencies is believed to enhance the learning process by ensuring that decision-making situations are repeated in sufficiently large numbers. According to Teece and colleagues, "If too many parameters are changed simultaneously, the ability of firms to conduct meaningful quasi experiments is attenuated."[32] Given the complexities of the learning process, the costs of learning in some cases may be lower for smaller specialized firms. Smaller firms may have the advantage of being able to allocate the majority of the resources available for learning and adaptation to a relatively small set of related production processes.[33]

Learning and core competencies have been shown to be important determinants of the performance of health care organizations. In health care settings, the learning process is to some extent evident in the positive association between procedure volume and outcomes (discussed in greater detail in the next section). For example, during our specialty hospital site visits, we consistently observed a culture supportive of coordination and cooperation aimed at achieving ongoing improvements in efficiency and quality. Specialty hospital managers generally attributed their success in process adaptation to three factors: relatively small size, which enables more rapid and efficient decision-making; flat hierarchical structures, which allow decision-making and process improvement to migrate to the most appropriate level; and focused and consistent management goals, which make it easier for team members to learn and practice their roles. Managers also emphasized the importance of performance feedback, mainly through surveys of customer satisfaction,[34] again indicating that their relatively small size allowed them to spend more time collecting, analyzing, and acting on customer feedback. While it is possible that diversified general hospitals are able to achieve similar learning effects, the smaller scale of specialty hospitals may lower the costs associated with learning.

In health care settings, there also appear to be distinct advantages to focusing production within core competencies.[35] Shortell, Morrison, and Hughes, in their three-year case study of eight large hospital systems, found that the best performing systems and hospitals were those that avoided diversification into unrelated activities, thereby minimizing diseconomies of scope and maximizing efficiencies associated with learning.[36] Eastaugh examined a panel of 219 U.S. acute-care hospitals from 1991 to 2000, finding that a 31 percent increase in specialization over the time period was associated with an 8 percent decline in costs per admission.[37] Douglas and Ryman reviewed and tested the theory of core competencies in hospitals using data from the thirty-two largest hospital markets in the United States. They found that the degree to which hospitals focused on core competencies was positively related to financial performance.[38]

In terms of core competencies, our site visits reached similar conclusions. When asked why their facilities performed one set of procedures or services and not another, managers consistently indicated that they had a strong desire not to venture too far from the core of their collective knowledge. Managers and owners emphasized that the key decision-makers are typically physician-owners, most of whom are likely to feel most comfortable focusing on the delivery of services in their specialty fields. One chief executive officer and physician-owner stressed that specialty hospitals often attract the most highly trained and skilled physicians in the community by allowing them essentially to redesign the care process based on the state of the art in their field. We found corroborating anecdotal evidence in the trade press.[39]

Impact of Specialty Hospitals

This section reviews the literature on the effects of specialty hospitals on costs, case mix, volume, quality, and competition. The primary sources of data are published literature, reports, the survey of specialty hospitals, and site visits to specialty hospitals.

The preceding discussion suggests that there are several areas in which specialty hospitals are likely to achieve production economies. First, specialty hospitals are able to take advantage of economies of scale and scope by producing relatively high volumes of a limited scope of services, and by lowering fixed costs by reengineering the care delivery process. Second, the site visits consistently found evidence of learning and core competencies. Managerial and clinical staff indicated a strong desire to focus on a relatively narrow array of tasks and indicated a commitment to perfecting those tasks. The evidence on scale and scope economies and core competencies suggests that there are efficiency reasons for some degree of diversification, but that expansion into unrelated activities can result in diminished financial performance. Specialty hospitals also may, in some cases, possess a technological advantage or resource that is unique in the market. This is likely to be the case for many entering specialty hospitals, as most have had the opportunity to redesign care delivery processes from the ground up.[40]

Perhaps as a result of these efficiencies, specialty hospitals appear to be capable of offering more intensive services for the same price. They tend to have substantially higher nurse-patient ratios[41] and to place greater emphasis on ancillary services identified by patients as important, such as comfortable, family-friendly rooms, more attention from administrative and clinical staff, and the mitigation of common inconveniences—by providing, for instance, appropriately located elevators and convenient parking. Specialty hospitals also appeal to physicians by offering newer equipment, more staff assistance, and more flexible operating room scheduling. These are costly services, yet specialty hospitals must compete for contracts with the same managed care organizations that general hospitals do; similar to general hospitals, they must also accept the Medicare fee schedule as payment in full.

There is some evidence that, on average, specialty hospitals treat patients with lower illness acuity compared to general hospitals.[42] These findings are consistent with the observed case-mix differences between ambulatory surgery centers and general hospitals.[43] The focused nature of specialty facilities may be better suited to patients whose care involves relatively little uncertainty, or whose conditions are reasonably well-defined. General hospitals may be more efficient in treating complex cases, particularly ones that allow them to exploit scope economies across service lines.

Several studies have found a positive association between the volume of services a hospital performs and the quality of the outcomes.[44] A criticism of specialty hospitals is that the volume of cases may be too low to capture the positive effects of volume on patient outcomes. Recent studies, however, show that specialty hospitals have *higher* procedural volumes compared to their general hospital counterparts. Cram and colleagues found that, compared to general hospitals, hospitals specializing in cardiac procedures had higher procedural volumes.[45] In addition, there is considerable debate over how much volume is necessary to improve outcomes. For example, a common belief is that outcomes for percutaneous coronary interventions are better in hospitals that perform more than 400 such procedures per year. Epstein and others, however, found that there were no significant mortality differences between hospitals with medium volume (200–399 cases per year) and high volume (400–999 cases per year). These findings suggest that specialty hospitals may be able to capture efficiencies associated with volume and learning-by-doing.[46]

Specialty hospitals appear to have outcomes that are at least as good as those of general hospitals. Dobson used Medicare Part A (MedPAR) data to compare eight MedCath heart hospitals to 1,056 peer general hospitals that perform open-heart surgery in the United States. After adjusting for risk of mortality, MedCath heart hospitals on average exhibited a 16 percent lower in-hospital mortality rate for Medicare cardiac cases than peer general hospitals.[47] Employing a different study design, Barro, Huckman, and Kessler also found that cardiac surgery outcomes were similar in markets with and without specialty hospitals.[48] Similarly, Cram, Rosenthal, and Vaughan-Sarrazin found no significant differences in mortality for cardiac patients treated at specialty hospitals and general hospitals, after adjusting for lower severity and higher procedure volume at specialty hospitals.[49] Analogous results have been found when comparing ambulatory surgery centers and general hospitals.[50] A comprehensive study commissioned by CMS and undertaken by RTI International reached similar conclusions, observing that "specialty hospitals provide generally high-quality care to satisfied patients."[51]

Specialty hospitals also reported relatively low patient-to-nurse ratios. The mean for surveyed hospitals was 3.4 patients per nurse (table 3-2), compared with, for example, a mean of 5.9 patients per nurse among general acute-care hospitals in California.[52] This difference suggests that specialty hospitals may be able to capture some of the positive quality and outcome effects associated with richer nurse staffing.[53]

Focusing on a limited number of services is also likely to increase accountability associated with those services. For example, a leader at one of the visited specialty hospitals remarked that "four procedures account for seventy percent of our business; if we develop any kind of quality problem in one or more of those procedures, it's a huge problem for our organization."[54] In addition, specialty hospitals typically engage in extensive collection of data on quality and patient satisfaction and use them to modify care processes.[55] Among the American Surgical Hospital Association (ASHA) member hospitals surveyed, 92 percent reported that they engaged in regular assessments of customer satisfaction (table 3-2). Finally, there is consistent anecdotal evidence that the kind of care delivered by the typical specialty hospital is consistent with the general trend toward "consumer-driven" health care.[56]

If specialty hospitals erode profits of general hospitals in the same market, we should observe lower or at least declining profit margins among general hospitals in markets where there is at least one specialty hospital.[57] In order to examine this issue, we statistically analyzed the extent to which

TABLE 3-2

MEANS AND STANDARD DEVIATIONS FOR SELECTED SURVEY ITEMS
FROM SPECIALTY HOSPITAL SAMPLE, 2004[a]

Variable	Mean	SD
Staffed inpatient beds	19.3	13.8
Percent of facilities with ER	42.1%	50.0%
Total number of facility owners	32.7	27.1
Number of physician-owners	31.6	23.2
Number of physician-owners admitting ≥ 5 patients/year	20.6	13.7
Percent with 0–1% ownership stake	33.6%	17.9%
Percent with 2–5% ownership stake	44.7%	9.2%
Percent with 6–9% ownership stake	12.4%	3.0%
Percent with ≥10% ownership stake	6.8%	1.9%
Inpatient discharges per year	835.1	796.9
Inpatient days per year	3,395.7	4,732.4
Inpatient surgeries (overnight stay) per year	717.7	512.7
Outpatient surgeries (no overnight stay) per year	3,105.5	2,849.0
Percent Medicare revenue	32.4%	19.1%
Percent Medicaid revenue	3.7%	3.8%
Percent commercial revenue	46.4%	25.1%
Percent other revenue	18.1%	20.5%
Percent revenue as charity care	2.1%	2.7%
Total taxes paid (previous tax year)	$1,924,830	$3,618,221
Patient-to-RN ratio	3.4	1.0
Percent w/patient satisfaction data	92.1%	27.3%

NOTES: a. Based on authors' survey of ASHA members conducted in 2004.

profit margins of general hospitals were affected by the presence of one or more specialty hospitals in the market. We obtained Medicare Hospital Cost Report (HCRIS) data for 1997 through 2003 for all U.S. acute-care hospitals.[58] For each hospital in the dataset, county and metropolitan statistical area (MSA) market areas were identified, and additional market-level data from the Bureau of Health Profession's Area Resource File (ARF)[59] were merged. Mean general hospital profit rates were calculated for all general hospitals in the sample.[60]

The analytical approach was to estimate what economists refer to as a profit function—a mathematical expression of the likely relationship among profit margin, the dependent variable, and the factors expected to affect profit margin.[61] We estimate a profit function of the following basic linear form (equation 3-1):

EQUATION 3-1

$$MARGIN_{it} = \alpha_0 + \alpha_1 D_{it} + \alpha_2 S_{it} + \alpha_3 P_{it} + \alpha_4 Z_{it} + \varepsilon_{it}.$$

In equation 3-1, $MARGIN_{it}$ refers to the operating margins of the ith general hospital in year t. Following Younis and Forgione, general hospital profit margins are a function of demand factors (D_{it}), supply factors (S_{it}), input prices (P_{it}), a vector of market area characteristics (Z_{it}), and an error term (ε_{it}) representing unexplained or unmeasured factors.[62] Demand factors included in the models are county-level per-capita income, population density, and unemployment rate. The last measure is included to capture the likely indigent-care burden faced by general hospitals. Supply factors include hospital bed size, length of stay, teaching status, cost per case, ownership status, inpatient discharges, outpatient visits per capita, and county-level physicians per 1,000 population. Price measures include the mean area wage for hospital workers[63] and the Medicare Part A (hospital) adjusted average per capita cost (AAPCC).

Among the main variables of interest are the indicator variables for specialty hospitals. We constructed two county-level variables, one measuring the presence of an established specialty hospital (in existence for at least two years), the other measuring the presence of a new specialty hospital (in existence for one year or less). Both measures were based on our survey of ASHA membership.

The other main variable of interest is a measure of market concentration. While not ideal, a standard method of measuring market concentration is the Herfindahl-Hirschman Index (HHI).[64] The HHI index equals 10,000 when an industry or market consists of a single seller. For the multivariate models of mean area profit rates, we assume the county to be the relevant geographic market.[65] In addition, since we are primarily interested in the effects of competition, we exclude from the analysis any county with only one acute-care hospital (that is, counties in which HHI = 10,000).

The model is specified as a fixed-effects panel data regression, which is designed to estimate the impact of the covariates on profit rates both cross-sectionally and over time.[66] An advantage of this approach is that it allows for the effects of specialty-hospital entry to accrue over time—effects that may not be observable looking only at a cross-sectional snapshot. It presents the problem, however, of the potential endogeneity of specialty-hospital entry; that is, specialty hospitals may be more likely to enter markets where general hospitals are earning relatively high operating margins.

To control for endogenous entry, we also estimate a two-stage model, where the entry of new specialty hospitals is modeled using instrumental variables. We select two variables—lagged mean county-level general-hospital operating margin and the presence of certificate-of-need regulation—as the primary instruments. In sum, we estimate four separate panel regression models for the seven-year time period 1997–2003:

- exogenous entry with hospital random effects;

- exogenous entry with hospital fixed effects;

- endogenous entry with hospital fixed effects (instruments are lagged mean county-level general-hospital profit margin and certificate-of-need status); and

- endogenous entry with hospital fixed effects, using state-level certificate-of-need status as an instrument.

Descriptive statistics for the sample are shown in table 3-3. Mean general hospital patient-care operating margins were negative and declining over the time period, consistent with other analyses of patient-care operating margins based on Medicare Cost Report data.[67] In 1997, only 1 percent of acute-care hospitals in the cohort were situated in counties with at least one specialty hospital. By 2003, the percentage had climbed to 9 percent. Three percent of acute-care hospitals resided in counties with at least one new specialty hospital, and 6 percent resided in counties with at least one

TABLE 3-3

MEANS OF HOSPITAL AND COUNTY-LEVEL VARIABLES, 1997 AND 2003

Variables	1997	2003
General hospital patient care profit margin	–0.0107	–0.0216
Any specialty hospital in county (0,1)	0.01	0.09
New specialty hospital in county (0,1)	0	0.03
Established specialty hospital in county (0,1)	0.01	0.06
General hospital concentration level (HHI)	3,604.66	3,806.04
General hospital inpatient beds per capita	0.16	2.03
Length of stay	5.31	4.91
Teaching status (0,1)	0.07	0.09
Mean general hospital cost per case	$18,323.20	$26,352.54
Hospital wage rate per hour	$16.48	$21.40
For-profit ownership status (0,1)	0.21	0.21
Number of inpatient discharges	6,797.45	9,148.38
Per-capita income	$25,385.59	$35,368.69
Population density (population per sq. mile)	1,880.60	1,758.06
Physicians per 1,000 population	2.28	2.32
Outpatient visits per capita	1.99	2.58
Inpatient admissions per 1,000 population	126.63	132.21
Medicare Part A AAPCC	$295.38	$322.38
Unemployment rate	5.00	2.89
1= CON present	0.63	0.53
Hospital bed size	189.42	212.42

SOURCES: Survey of ASHA membership, Medicare HCRIS cost reports, Bureau of Labor Statistics (BLS), and U.S. Department of Health and Human Services (2004).
NOTE: Sample sizes vary according to missing data in each year. Sample sizes for general hospital patient care profit margin are the following: 1997 (2,112); 1998 (3,441); 1999 (3,451); 2000 (3,425); 2001 (3,315); 2002 (3,131); and 2003 (2,306).

established specialty hospital. Operating margins of general hospitals differed in markets with and without specialty hospitals (figure 3-1).

The results of the four multivariable regression models are reported in table 3-4. For each model, the unit of observation is the general hospital, and the dependent variable is general-hospital operating margins. The first

FIGURE 3-1

TRENDS IN GENERAL HOSPITAL PROFIT MARGINS: U.S. COUNTIES
WITH SPECIALTY HOSPITALS COMPARED TO U.S. COUNTIES
WITHOUT SPECIALTY HOSPITALS, 1997–2003

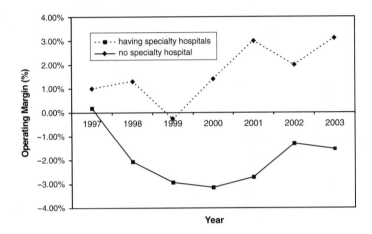

SOURCE: Authors' analysis of Medicare Cost Report data (CMS 2006a) by county.

column shows the results of the exogenous entry with hospital random effects. The random-effects model estimates parameters for all covariates, including time-invariant factors.

All of the covariates have the expected signs. Teaching status has a negative effect on operating margins, mainly because while teaching hospitals typically have higher operating costs, many payers face the same price schedules as they would at nonteaching hospitals. Payment mechanisms are also likely to play a role in the observed positive association between cost per case (that is, average cost) and profit margins. Hospitals continue to be paid by some third-party payers on a fee-for-service (FFS) or cost-plus basis. Thus, at least for FFS patients, a positive relationship between costs and profits is expected.

However, we also included an exogenous county-level, wage-rate variable (WAGE) to account for the contamination of the cost-per-case variable by payment-mechanism effects. As expected, wage rates for health care workers in the county have a significant negative effect on general-hospital operating margins. It is likely that the measure of per-capita income is also

TABLE 3-4

PANEL-DATA GENERAL HOSPITAL PROFIT FUNCTION
REGRESSION MODELS, 1997–2003

Independent Variable	(1)	(2)	(3)	(4)
Hospital bed size	0.00002010	—	0.00000618	0.00000648
Length of stay	0.00088330	0.00159820	0.00026110	0.00011250
1= teaching hospital	-0.06994830[b]	—	—	—
Cost per case	0.00000002[b]	0.00000002[b]	0.00000002[b]	0.00000002[b]
Hospital wage rate per hour	-0.00080760[a]	-0.00175150[b]	-0.00154290[b]	-0.00199730[b]
1= for-profit hospital	0.09089290[b]	—	—	—
Number of discharges	0.00000294[b]	0.00000177[b]	0.00000149[b]	0.00000119[a]
Per-capita income	-0.00000104[b]	-0.00000154[b]	0.00000001	-0.00000006
Population density	-0.00000192[b]	0.00000468	0.00000998[b]	0.00001020[b]
MDs per 1,000 pop.	0.00290340[b]	-0.00042080	0.00234720	0.00284090
Outpatient visits per capita	-0.00048780	0.00002220	0.00004150	0.00022630
Medicare Part A AAPCC	0.00008420[b]	0.00024170[b]	-0.00002110	-0.00002690
Unemployment rate	-0.00125450[b]	-0.00040910	-0.00031000	0.00028860
1= CON present	0.01000060[b]	0.03585260[b]	—	—
HHI	0.00000269[b]	0.00000076	0.00000148	0.00000059
1= new SCP present	0.00391660	0.00813150	0.19520800[a]	0.39811130[b]
1= established SCP present	0.02097670[b]	0.02913170[b]	0.06328550[b]	0.10592820[b]
Constant	-0.06905830	-0.06822490	-0.03755700	0.02790180
Number of observations	18,506	18,506	16,192	16,192
Number of groups	3,453	3,453	3,118	3,118
R-squared	0.0868	0.0090	0.0074	0.0050
F / Wald Chi-square	544.82	9.79	52.56	48.30
P value	< 0.0001	< 0.0001	< 0.0001	< 0.0001

SOURCES: Based on data from a survey of ASHA membership (2004), Centers for Medicare and Medicaid Services HCRIS cost reports (2006a) (see chapter 3), Bureau of Labor Statistics (BLS) wage data (2004), and U.S. Department of Health and Human Services (2004).

NOTES: The four models are: (1) exogenous entry with hospital random effects; (2) exogenous entry with hospital fixed effects; (3) endogenous entry with hospital fixed effects, instruments are lagged mean county-level general hospital profit margin and certificate-of-need status; and (4) endogenous entry with hospital fixed effects, instrument is certificate-of-need status.

a. Significant at $p \leq 0.10$ (t-test).

b. Significant at $p \leq 0.05$ (t-test).

approximating area wages, reflected in its negative association with profit margins. Tax status (1 = for-profit) has a significantly positive effect on operating margins, which is expected, given that the earning of profits is normally an explicit goal of for-profit hospitals. The number of discharges also has a positive and significant association with profits, perhaps reflecting a combination of fee-schedule payment mechanisms and synergies between growth-oriented managerial strategies and margins. Finally, as expected, significant positive associations are observed for physicians per population and Medicare Part-A AAPCC.

The remaining rows show the results for the variables of interest. The presence of CON laws is positively associated with general-hospital operating margins in the random- and fixed-effects exogenous entry models (the CON variable was dropped from the endogenous models because it was used as an instrument). The positive relationship between entry barriers and higher operating margins is generally expected. The HHI also has a positive association with operating margins, as expected, but the magnitude of the coefficient is small in the random-effects model and not significantly different from zero at $p \leq 0.05$ in the other models. The specialty-hospital indicator variables suggest an unanticipated effect: The presence of established specialty hospitals in the market appears to be associated with higher general-hospital operating margins, even in the endogenous entry models. New specialty hospitals are also associated with higher general-hospital operating margins, but only in the endogenous entry models.[68]

Policy Implications

The debate over specialty hospitals has raised several policy questions, two of which have received a high level of attention. First, do specialty hospitals harm the ability of general hospitals to provide indigent care? Some argue that specialty hospitals take profitable business away from general hospitals, and, as general hospitals lose market share, particularly in high-margin product lines, they are hampered in their ability to provide low-margin services and meet their implied obligations to serve the community. Second, does having an ownership stake in the facility create financial incentives for physicians to provide inappropriate and unnecessary treatment? What are the optimal policy options to address these questions? Rather than make explicit recommendations, we discuss some of the salient economic issues concerning these two problems.

In this section, policies are discussed in terms of their effectiveness in accomplishing intended objectives. In order to assess the net effect of a policy, ideally it is necessary to take into account all direct and indirect effects attributable to it. The sum of these effects is analogous to what economists refer to as change in net social welfare—that is, the extent to which the policy affects aggregate well-being. For example, the Federal Trade Commission recently emphasized that health care policies intended to mitigate some of the less desirable side effects of competition must be weighed against the losses normally resulting from restrictions on market entry and competition.[69]

The indigent-care issue has several components. The first has to do with the practice on the part of general hospitals of meeting their implicit obligation to serve the community[70] by cross-subsidizing low-margin services with high-margin services, combined with other government subsidies. Many of the former state rate-regulation programs were explicitly designed to help acute-care hospitals meet these obligations;[71] however, all but one were dismantled during the 1990s. In the absence of state rate regulation, hospitals have relied on six other mechanisms to pay for unprofitable services:

- tax-deductible donations,

- tax-exempt bond financing,

- exemption from income and property taxes,

- internal cross-subsidization,

- Medicaid disproportionate share payments (additional payment for treating a disproportionate share of Medicaid patients), and

- state-administered charity-care risk pools (figure 3-2).[72]

Tax exemption is perhaps the most widespread subsidy provided to nonprofit general hospitals. Nonprofit tax status allows hospitals to avoid property and income tax in exchange for an obligation to serve the community. However, Kane and Wubbenhorst found that the amount of

FIGURE 3-2

NONPROFIT GENERAL-HOSPITAL METHODS FOR FUNDING INDIGENT CARE

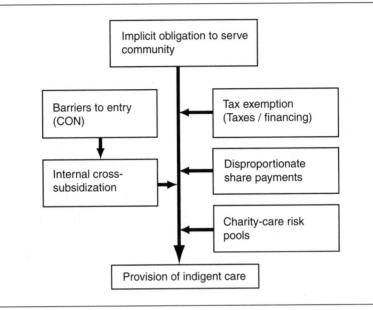

SOURCE: Authors' review of the literature.

charity care provided by hospitals is significantly less than the amount of tax benefit accrued through nonprofit status.[73] Thus, even if tax exemption were the only means for hospitals to fund indigent care, the amount of the benefit on average appears to be more than sufficient to fund prevailing levels. Although specialty hospitals generally provide less charity care per facility (approximately 2.1 percent of gross patient-care revenues; table 3-2), they contribute on average approximately $2 million annually in state and federal taxes. This represents an additional 5.1 percent of gross patient-care revenues. The combined 7.2 percent of gross patient-care revenues exceeds the average charity-care provision of tax-exempt general hospitals, which is approximately 5–6 percent of revenues.[74] Similarly, Greenwald and colleagues report that specialty hospitals provide more net community benefits than their not-for-profit competitors, and that "the higher community benefits generated by specialty hospitals were attributable almost entirely to the taxes they paid as for-profit entities."[75]

Hospital internal cross-subsidization is to be distinguished from the popular notion that hospitals shift costs between third-party payers; that is, "one group pays more because another pays less."[76] In this case, hospitals cross-subsidize low-margin indigent services with the proceeds from high-margin services. Under normal circumstances, internal cross-subsidization would not be sustainable, mainly because sustained high margins on some services would encourage market entry, and as firms entered, the excess profits would be competed away.[77] In order for cross-subsidization to work, government must restrict market entry, either through certificate-of-need or some other means. Indeed, that is how many states currently approach the problem, and an important reason Congress has resorted to the specialty-hospital moratorium.

There are at least two problems with policies encouraging cross-subsidization of this kind. First, the policy relies on CON to limit market entry, and there is a large volume of research critical of CON.[78] As discussed in chapter 2, studies of the impact of CON programs have consistently found them to be ineffective at controlling costs and enhancing access. Sloan and Steinwald found that mature CON programs had an insignificant effect on hospital costs, and immature CON programs actually increased costs.[79] Studies by Lanning, Morrisey, and Ohsfeldt and by Antel, Ohsfeldt, and Becker also concluded that CON is associated with higher inpatient costs and expenditures per capita.[80] A possible explanation is that the CON constraint prevents hospitals from employing the least-cost combination of inputs to produce inpatient services, resulting in allocative inefficiency.[81] Further, there is no evidence that the repeal of CON was associated with an increase in hospital expenditures. As a result of the apparent failure of CON to achieve its stated goals, many state CON programs have either been terminated or significantly reformed since the repeal of the Health Planning Act in 1986.[82] It would be more difficult in theory for hospitals located in competitive markets in non-CON states to engage in internal cross-subsidization; instead, they would have to rely on tax exemption, disproportionate share payments, and charity-care risk pools to fund indigent care.

Second, it is not clear whether the losses in net social welfare associated with restricting market entry exceed the costs of alternative means of ensuring the provision of indigent care, such as direct subsidies. The Federal Trade Commission's recent report on health care competition integrated this point into one of its policy recommendations, emphasizing that "[competition] does not work well when certain facilities are expected to cross-subsidize uncompensated care. In general, it is more efficient to provide subsidies directly to those who should receive them, rather than to obscure cross subsidies and indirect subsidies in transactions that are not transparent."[83] There is general agreement that, economic tradeoffs notwithstanding, the existing reliance on indirect subsidies is precarious and unstable.[84] In addition, the Institute of Medicine (IOM) comprehensive report on safety-net providers and systems in the United States called for "a targeted federal initiative" that "should concentrate on both the infrastructure for [indigent] care and subsidies for the care itself."[85] The U.S. experience with airline regulation provides an excellent example. In order to develop air travel infrastructure, airline regulation required carriers to cross-subsidize unprofitable routes with profitable ones. Cross-subsidization appeared to contribute to infrastructure development in the early years of regulation, but eventually it led to high costs.[86] Consumer welfare and producer surplus improved markedly following deregulation.[87] If subsidizing indigent care is a policy objective, the economically optimal public policy would be to subsidize any hospital directly for providing indigent care.[88] Protecting incumbent hospitals from competitive entry may be just as likely to allow incumbent firms to maintain higher prices and facilitate slack in organizational processes, rather than permit them to fund additional indigent care.

A related concern is that specialty hospitals engage in unfair competition with general hospitals by taking only less severe and more profitable cases—that is, by cream-skimming. As noted, there is some evidence that specialty hospitals, like their ambulatory surgery center predecessors, treat healthier patients with fewer comorbid conditions. However, from a policy perspective, treating healthier patients in less intensive settings is likely to improve patient welfare, given the extensive literature on the cost and quality benefits associated with triaging patients from inpatient to outpatient settings following the implementation of Medicare's PPS. Thus, the cream-skimming issue, as others have observed, is predominantly a function of, first, variation in operating margins within DRGs, and, second, crude case-mix adjustments in current reimbursement rates. Case-mix adjustment methodology has improved dramatically in recent years, and CMS maintains the administrative data necessary for such adjustments.[89] Again, according to economic theory, establishing administered prices that are more closely aligned with average costs, together with improvements in case-mix adjustment, would be superior policy mechanisms compared to restrictions on market entry.

In sum, there are significant drawbacks to the current four-part strategy to encourage the provision of indigent care. Tax exemption should, in theory, provide sufficient compensation for indigent care, particularly when combined with disproportionate share payments and charity-care risk pools. However, there are no explicit mechanisms in place to control how hospitals allocate the proceeds from tax exemption. Internal cross-subsidization would not be sustainable in competitive markets; therefore, it must be accompanied by costly entry-barrier regulations. Both of these policies are suboptimal insofar as they result in net losses in social welfare that are likely to exceed the value of indigent care delivered. Policies such as direct subsidies for indigent care and more accurate case-mix adjustment of payments would likely result in overall gains in net social welfare.

The remaining policy issue involves the potential effects of physician self-referral. The costs and benefits of this practice have been debated for many years, mainly because the dominant physician payment mechanism in the United States has been and continues to be fee-for-service, which creates financial incentives for self-referral. In the case of specialty hospitals, the general argument is that physicians may have financial incentives to admit patients to facilities in which they have an ownership stake. This argument is, to some extent, based on research that has found utilization of ancillary services higher when an ownership relationship exists between referring physicians and the services.[90] However, there are at least five important limitations to applying these arguments to acute-care hospitals:

- The vast majority of studies of higher utilization resulting from self-referral are based on physician ownership of *ancillary* services, rather than acute-care hospitals. Mitchell and Sass, in their frequently cited study of physician referral, failed to find higher utilization rates associated with self-referral to acute-care hospitals.[91] This lack of association has been one of the main reasons that the two phases of Stark anti-kickback legislation[92] have exempted physician ownership of acute-care hospitals.[93] In addition, there is no direct evidence that the observed higher utilization rates resulting from self-referral to ancillary services represent inappropriate or unnecessary care.[94]

- There is no direct evidence that physician self-referral is motivated disproportionately by financial incentives. Physician self-referral is motivated by four factors: appropriateness, quality, efficiency, and financial returns. The relative magnitude of each of these incentives has been the subject of debate, but there is no direct evidence to suggest how, on average, physicians assign weights to each factor. Consistent with the empirical findings, anecdotal evidence suggests that physicians may disproportionately weight financial incentives when the referral is for standardized products or services, such as lab or pharmacy, and disproportionately weight appropriateness and quality when the referral is for more intensive procedures, such as surgery.[95]

- There is no evidence that self-referrals result in worse outcomes than other types of referral.[96] A likely reason for these findings is the endogeneity of three factors: physician quality, the likelihood of self-referral, and the quality of patient outcomes. Site visits and trade-press literature indicate that physician investors in specialty hospitals tend to be those who highly value efficiency in the quality and cost dimensions. Thus, for many physician investors, self-referral is likely to represent the optimal referral in terms of quality and cost.

- In the case of physician ownership of acute-care facilities, it is likely that the magnitude of financial incentives is limited. The U.S. General Accounting Office found that 30 percent of specialty hospitals surveyed had no physician investors.[97] For half of the facilities with physician investors, the average individual physician-ownership share was less than 2 percent. In the ASHA survey, nearly 80 percent of physician investors owned 5 percent or less (table 3-2). Moreover, the entrepreneurial return (that is, the fraction of the facility fee considered operating margin) for any single case is likely to be substantially less than the professional fee charged by physicians. Given the order of magnitude difference between these two revenue streams, physician incentives are likely to be driven more by professional fees, which do not vary significantly by practice setting, than by entrepreneurial returns.[98] Indeed, in this context the potential for a surgeon to enhance his or her own productivity is a more likely source of financial incentive for self-referral to a specialty hospital. In other words, the primary financial motivation may be to enhance the return on investment for the surgeon's investment in "human capital" (associated with the number of procedures performed) rather than any effort to assure a return on investment in the form of financial assets (associated with the overall financial performance of the hospital).

- There is often a double standard applied when judging the wisdom of physician self-referral. For example, a recent *Wall Street Journal* editorial observed that "about 90 percent of the primary-care doctors in southwestern Wisconsin are owned by the hospitals" and that "the reason so many hospitals own primary-care physicians is so that they can direct referrals into their own hospitals."[99] Although the main reasons for hospital-physician integration may also include factors such as reduction in transaction costs, improvements in efficiency, and bargaining clout with managed care organizations,[100] there is a widespread belief that such hospital vertical integration into physician groups is a means to direct referrals to hospitals, consistent with the concerns expressed in the *Wall Street Journal*.[101]

In terms of policy options, even if we were to assume that these limitations were not important, a more central question is whether creating barriers to market entry is the most appropriate means of addressing the issue. The net social welfare losses associated with barriers to market entry are likely to be greater than those attributable to physician referral incentives, particularly in light of the weakness of those incentives.

Concluding Remarks

In this chapter we have reviewed the theory and evidence pertaining to some of the key characteristics of specialty hospitals, including efficiency, demand, case mix, and quality. These findings were supported by observations from five site visits to specialty hospitals. We also conducted statistical analyses of the effects of specialty hospitals on the profit margins of general hospitals. The main findings of the study can be briefly summarized as follows:

First, there are economic advantages associated with specialization, due mainly to process redesign, learning, avoidance of diseconomies of scope, and focus on core competencies. Specialty hospitals appear to have equal or better patient outcomes compared to their general-hospital counterparts. Hence, there is no evidence to suggest that specialty hospitals should be barred from entering acute inpatient care markets on the basis of efficiency or quality of care.

Second, there is no evidence, other than anecdotal, to suggest that general hospitals have been financially harmed by competition from specialty hospitals, or that such competition is undesirable from a societal perspective. Specialty hospitals compete with general hospitals in the same manner in which general hospitals compete with each other. Based on a longitudinal study of general-hospital profit margins in markets with and without specialty hospitals, we find that profit margins of general hospitals have not been affected by the entry of specialty hospitals. Contrary to the conjecture that entry by specialty hospitals erodes the overall operating profits of general hospitals, general hospitals residing in markets with at least one specialty hospital have higher profit margins than those that do not compete with specialty hospitals. These findings are also consistent with economic theory, which suggests that firms will enter markets in which extant profit margins are comparatively higher.

Third, though often cited as a significant policy concern, there is no evidence that physician self-referral is a problem in specialty hospitals. Physician self-referral is likely to play a relatively minor role in patient utilization of specialty hospitals because physicians' ownership interests tend to be small, and the associated financial incentive to use the specialty hospital is small and indirect relative to the larger and more direct financial incentive from the professional fee for providing the service itself.

4

Competition in Health Insurance Markets: The Case of Managed Care Reform

The discussion of specialty hospitals in the previous chapter illustrates some of the impediments to relying on market forces to organize and allocate health care resources. A similar impediment, in some cases, is the regulation of health insurers. One of the most active areas of government regulation in recent years has been the regulation of managed care organizations and health plans. Just as the last vestiges of classic, utility-style regulation are giving way to regulatory reform—and, in some cases, complete deregulation—throughout the economy, state and federal legislators over the past decade have increasingly viewed managed care regulation as the next best alternative to a national health system. For example, during a 2001 California Senate Insurance Committee hearing addressing health plan representatives, State Senator Jackie Speier stated emphatically, "With more than 24 million people enrolled in managed care in California, you can't tell me that [health plans] should be treated any differently than any other public utility."[1] In her comments, Senator Speier invoked the public interest rationale for economic regulation simply by emphasizing the number of California residents affected by managed care, which involves roughly 70 percent of the state population. Senator Speier's public utility thoughts have been shared by other industry observers.[2]

State enactment of managed care regulations has diffused rapidly in the United States during the previous decade.[3] Many states have enacted at least some form of legislation controlling various aspects of managed care business practices. Regulations typically address two concerns: the content of the benefit package offered by health plans (that is, coverage mandates, such as cancer screenings), and the operations of health plans

78

(such as restrictions on the exclusion criteria for provider networks). As contracts between health plans and providers become more complex and widespread,[4] state legislators are likely to view health plan operations increasingly as an entry point for regulations. Whereas the economic effects of regulation in general are well understood, the application of that body of knowledge to managed care regulation is considerably less developed.

The goal of this chapter is to apply the economic theory of regulation to managed care regulation. There is a large body of literature on the costs and benefits of economic regulation in industries other than health care, such as airlines and telecommunications. Some studies have applied the literature on the economics of regulation to hospitals,[5] but few have applied the theory to managed care regulation. Throughout the debates on the scope and breadth of new managed care regulations, two questions remain largely unanswered. First, to what extent do current forms of managed care regulation resemble classic economic regulation? Second, are there specific lessons from the forty-year experience with economic regulation (and, in many industries, deregulation) that are relevant to current debates over the form and scope of managed care regulation? These questions are explored in the first section of the chapter. The second section reviews aspects of the economic theory of regulation relevant to managed care regulation, and the third applies the theory to managed care regulation. The remaining sections provide discussion and conclusions.

Economic Regulation

During the forty years from 1930 to 1970, the United States government enacted more new regulations and created more regulatory agencies than at any time in its history.[6] Regulatory agencies focused primarily on controlling public utilities, such as water, electricity, natural gas, telecommunications, transportation, insurance, and banking. These industries were believed to be "affected by the public interest," although the operational definition of public interest was debated extensively in the courts.[7] The primary administrative control mechanism used by regulators was an assortment of instruments referred to collectively as economic regulation, the core features of which include an agency charged with overseeing a private industry and employing administrative controls on capacity, quality, costs, or profits, or some combination of these.[8] Economic regulation is often observed in industries where markets fail to operate freely and competitively, or where the attributes of the markets, products, or services add layers of relatively high complexity to transacting and contracting among producers and consumers. Complexity typically stems from the presence of uncertainty and imperfect information, production and consumption externalities, the need for cross-subsidization, investments in non-redeployable assets, and excessive market power. One or more of these attributes has been observed in virtually all industries in which economic regulation has been featured, and two are relevant to managed care regulation: uncertainty and imperfect information, and excessive market power.

Uncertainty and imperfect information can lead to difficulties evaluating contractual performance and product and service attributes (that is, price and quality). Information problems have figured prominently in various kinds of consumer protection regulations, such as those enforced by the Food and Drug Administration and other agencies charged with overseeing product and service quality.[9] Another potential source of an "unfair playing field" is the presence of excessive or unusual market power. Market power figures prominently in the regulation of traditional public utilities (such as water), where granting exclusive service privileges to a single firm exposes consumers to monopoly output and pricing. Economic regulation is a means of establishing and enforcing nonmonopoly prices and output.

In most cases, relatively complex transactions are more efficiently organized in settings that feature administrative controls.[10] Depending on the magnitude of the additional costs and difficulties associated with more complex transactions, "first best" (that is, cost-minimizing or most efficient) organization may take the form of economic regulation, where regulatory agencies administer implicit contracts between producers and consumers.[11] The regulatory agent must determine the appropriate protection for the producers' right to serve consumers and the consumers' right to be served by the producers. Protecting the producers' right to serve includes securing investments in non-redeployable assets, devising flexible pricing mechanisms, and assuring firm solvency. Consumers' right to be served must be protected from monopoly output levels, price uncertainty, service holdup, access denial, and quality shading.

Rate and capacity regulation are means of administering the dual contract. Given the duality of the contract and a political structure that allows input from all sides, however, interested parties have the potential to gain from regulation by strategically influencing the regulatory process.[12] In administering contracts between producers and consumers, the regulator allocates resources until the marginal political support for any regulatory policy change generates no additional increase in political support.[13] In addition to consumers, producers, and other special-interest groups, the regulatory process can also be influenced by motivated legislative champions and issue networks comprised of technical specialists, journalists, administrators, foundations, and political entrepreneurs.[14]

The cumulative knowledge suggests, rather consistently across studies and industries, that the imposition of economic regulation on an industry results in higher costs and prices than would have been observed in its absence.[15] Deregulation occurred in many of the formerly regulated industries as the costs of regulatory governance began to exceed the costs of nonregulatory governance. The relative costs of regulatory governance increased as, first, some of the underlying market problems that led to regulation abated; second, agencies faced increasingly difficult administrative tasks; and third, financial control mechanisms, such as rate-of-return regulation (where allowable operating margins, revenues, or costs are established by the regulators) caused regulated firms to use inefficient mixes of inputs.[16] Applications of price controls in various components of the health care industry have also been found to cause distortions in prices and costs.[17]

These effects were in part observable in post-deregulation data from the industries of power (electricity and natural gas), transportation (railroads, trucking, airlines), and financial services. In the wake of regulatory reform, many of these industries experienced significant (10–30 percent) decreases in real prices and net operating costs.[18] In addition to efficiency gains, many of the industries subjected to economic regulation achieved improvements in quality, safety, and access following deregulation.[19]

Managed Care Regulation

At the time of their inception in the mid-1970s, managed care organizations were regulated differently than indemnity insurers, with less emphasis on financial requirements and more emphasis on the scope of coverage and the impact of health plan organization on the provision of care.[20] The late 1990s was a time of resurgence for managed care regulation, driven mainly by dissatisfaction on the part of consumers and providers over the limitations that health plans placed on the provision of medical care.[21] The backlash was likely made worse as indemnity plans exited the market or became too expensive for most employers and individuals, thereby leaving many with little choice but reluctantly to join managed care plans.[22] Currently, most states have implemented some form of managed care quality or operations regulation.[23] Examples of these regulations are shown in table 4-1.

The implicit theory underlying most managed care regulations is that, if left uncontrolled, the business practices of managed care organizations will tend to trade off quality and access in order to increase revenue and profits; consequently, the arguments go, managed care organizations will fall short of providing the socially optimal level of care. This is due in part to the prevalence of prepaid contractual mechanisms in managed care, such as administered prices and capitation. The extent to which prepaid contracts lead to problems depends on the complexity of the transaction. Relatively high levels of uncertainty and information imperfections common to health care transactions are likely to result in "incomplete" contracts between health plans, providers, and enrollees.[24]

The prevalence of incomplete contracting opens the door to opportunistic behavior *ex post*, examples of which may include skimping (on the part of plans), moral hazard (on the part of enrollees and providers), and, in some cases, fraud. The existence of unusually high levels of uncertainty and information imperfections also increases search costs for consumers (choosing plans and providers) and providers (choosing plan/network affiliations). Uncertainty and information imperfections, and resultant incomplete contracts, provide the rationale for the vast majority of extant managed care regulations.[25] Most of the remaining regulations are attempts to counteract perceived asymmetries in bargaining power among purchasers, health plans, providers, and enrollees.

TABLE 4-1
EXAMPLES OF STATE AND FEDERAL MANAGED CARE REGULATIONS

Health Plan Operations	Coverage Mandates
Provider access to plan networks	Preventive care
Plan/provider solvency requirements	Reconstructive surgery
Physician-enrollee communication	Pain management
Continuity of care	Mental health
Plan-provider dispute resolution	Contraceptives
Plan-enrollee dispute resolution	Management of chronic diseases
Consumer complaint procedures	Experimental treatments
Out-of-area/emergency coverage	Second opinions
Minimum lengths of hospital stay	Standing specialist referrals
Quality audits and reporting	End-of-life care
External review	Clinical trials
Health plan liability	
Administered plan–provider contracts	
Provider antitrust waivers	

SOURCES: Anders (2001); Butler (1999); Rogal and Stenger (2001); Zelman (1999).

Consider the case of managed care regulation in California. During the fourteen years from 1990 to 2004, California enacted more than 180 distinct managed care regulations (figure 4-1).[26] These laws are in addition to California's Knox-Keene Health Care Service Plan Act of 1975, which enacted an extensive set of rules aimed at the operations of prepaid health plans and transferred regulatory authority of prepaid plans from the attorney general to the Department of Corporations.[27] Many of the laws and regulations enacted during the 1990–2001 period were amendments and addenda to the Knox-Keene Act.

The process through which the activities of special-interest groups and issue networks result in managed care laws and regulations in California is complex and difficult to generalize about. However, some basic facts can be drawn from press releases and other public records generated during the legislative debates. Purchasers are concerned about the quality of the health

FIGURE 4-1

CUMULATIVE NUMBER OF MANAGED CARE ORGANIZATION
LAWS AND REGULATIONS ENACTED IN CALIFORNIA, 1990–2004

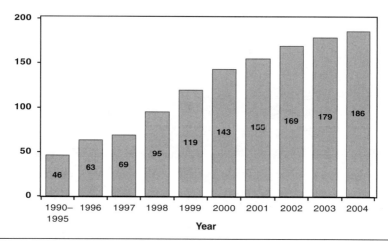

SOURCES: Authors' analysis based on data from California Association of Health Plans (1997–2001) and legislation listed and described at the Legislative Council of California's website www.leginfo. ca.gov (last accessed January 15, 2006).

care they get for their money, but they are also highly attuned to the overall cost of providing coverage to their employees and members, and how inflation in health insurance premiums compares to inflation in other inputs.[28] Representing the interests of large employers, the California Chamber of Commerce focuses primarily on how much proposed legislation or regulatory rules will end up costing purchasers. Similarly, the Pacific Business Group on Health (PBGH) devotes considerable effort to collecting and disseminating quality-related information to its constituents; but members continue to be concerned about costs.[29]

Given that health plans enroll the vast majority of their customers through employer groups and government purchasers, the policy interests of health plans often correspond with those of purchasers. Provider groups, such as the California Medical Association (CMA), the California Association of Physician Organizations (CAPO), and the California Healthcare Association (CHA),[30] often align themselves with consumer groups, and are more likely to support legislation and regulatory rules that result in greater physician autonomy, broader scope of covered services, timely payment of claims, and higher payment rates.[31] Accordingly, there exists a fundamental tension between providers, who generally want more money put into the system, and payers, who generally want less money in the system.

Economic Regulation and Managed Care

To what extent do current forms of managed care regulation resemble economic regulation? The majority of managed care laws resemble those employed in other regulated industries. Most are targeted at mitigating the effects of uncertainty and information imperfections. Among extant laws aimed at governing health plan operations, bargaining asymmetry provides nominal justification for those laws aimed at enrollee access to providers, provider access to health plan networks, and other laws targeted at health plan and provider contracting. The other operations laws are nominally designed to increase the amount of information available to purchasers, enrollees, plans, and providers, and to provide mechanisms to settle disputes arising from incomplete contracting.

Although they represent a relatively small proportion of managed care regulatory activity, laws governing provider contracting have received a great deal of attention, particularly in California. For example, two bills under consideration by the California legislature in 1999 involved a significant escalation in government oversight of rates and the processes through which health plans pay provider groups. One would have required plans to file evidence that capitation rates paid to provider groups were based on actuarial estimates; submitted rates would have been subject to review. A similar bill created the new Department of Managed Health Care (DMHC), which was nominally charged with, among other oversight activities, ensuring provider solvency. In debates during the deliberations of the DMHC's Fiscal Solvency Standards Board over how the department would fulfill those obligations, the notion of reviewing and approving health plan capitation rates paid to providers received serious consideration.

Laws intended to govern the scope of benefit packages are, in general, aimed at formalizing and explicating incomplete contractual terms between enrollees and plans, with the intent to reduce uncertainty in the scope and depth of coverage. However, laws mandating coverage also implicitly address bargaining asymmetry to the extent that mandates align with specific provider groups—for example, mental health parity laws and mental health providers. In these cases, mandated benefits have the secondary effect of compelling plans to include specific provider subgroups in their networks.

There have been relatively few studies examining the effects of managed care regulations on costs and quality. Laws intended to govern the scope of benefit packages share the nominal intent to improve quality, but the extent to which those laws are capable of doing so and the extent to which they have succeeded (and at what cost) are unclear, for four reasons. First, there is some evidence to suggest that mandated coverage of certain kinds of preventive care (such as cancer screenings) may be beneficial in the long run due to the access barriers created by the relatively high price-elasticity of demand for those services.[32] However, when subjected to rigorous cost-effectiveness analyses, many preventive services tend to show no consistent patterns and often yield perverse findings, such as some cancer screenings that cost over $1 billion per life-year saved.[33] The cost-effectiveness ratios for other mandated benefits are equally uncertain. Some studies have estimated added costs associated with a typical assortment of mandates ranging from 3 to 15 percent of health insurance premiums, with little evidence of incremental quality increases attributable to the laws.[34]

Second, it is difficult to disentangle anecdote from evidence in assessing the extent of quality-related problems attributable to health plans and managed care organizations. Numerous empirical studies have found that managed health plans appear to provide care comparable to or better than their unmanaged counterparts.[35] Studies conducted before and after the diffusion of state regulations reached similar conclusions. As a result, it is likely that some managed care regulations address problems that are perceived rather than real.[36]

Third, quality regulation is not exempt from the same kinds of distortions common to rate regulation. For example, whereas rate regulation encouraged airlines to compete away excess profits through nonprice (quality) competition,[37] quality regulation may encourage health plans and provider groups essentially to compete away excess quality through price competition, even if the excess quality has value to some purchasers and enrollees.[38]

Finally, mandated benefits force employers to purchase a minimum benefit package that may differ from what they would be willing to pay for in an unregulated market, thereby compelling them to pass the costs of the richer benefit package on to employees in the form of lower net wages.[39] There is also likely to be an adverse selection effect as healthier enrollees drop coverage at the higher prices.

Similar to laws aimed at the scope of benefit packages, there are positive and negative aspects of laws aimed at health plan operations. As has been the case in other industries, there is general agreement that laws aimed at increasing the overall level of available information and decreasing search costs generally have positive effects and, in the long run, the potential to improve quality and reduce costs.[40] Examples include plan and provider reporting requirements (such as financial reporting, solvency standards, and medical error reporting), plan and provider quality audits, prohibition of plan restrictions on provider–patient communication (such as "gag clauses"), and disclosure of "evidence of coverage." There are also likely to be net benefits from laws aimed at continuity of care, which typically allow patients to continue seeing their physicians for a limited time even if the provider is no longer a network participant. Other operations laws are intended simply to clarify what is covered and what is not, thereby reducing the level of contractual ambiguity among plans, providers, and enrollees.

Many managed care laws, however, have been shown to add significant costs to health plans while being of questionable value to enrollees. Examples include minimum lengths of stay for certain procedures (such as maternity stays) and patients, health plan liability, independent external review of coverage decisions, administered plan–provider contracts (including regulated payment rates), provider network restrictions, and provider antitrust exemptions. A typical assortment of these laws is estimated to add 3–14 percent to plan premiums.[41] Laws intended to regulate payments from plans to providers, regulate plan premiums, or grant providers exemptions from antitrust laws have been estimated to increase premiums another 10–20 percent.[42]

Discussion

What lessons can we learn from the economic regulation of other industries? The preceding discussion points to four lessons. First, it is very important for lawmakers to reassess continuously the need for regulation, and be prepared to deregulate whenever appropriate. This requires assessing more than simply the relative costs and benefits of specific regulations. The real issue is whether the overall costs of regulatory governance—which include the costs of specific regulations in addition to the costs of administering regulatory programs—exceed the costs of nonregulatory governance. In the case of managed care regulation, there is ample opportunity to conduct such research, given the relatively high level of heterogeneity in the design, scope, and enforcement of regulation across states. In California, the vast majority of managed care laws were passed in the absence of economic impact estimates *ex ante* or assessments from other states *ex post*.

A closely related lesson is that economic regulations should be targeted at real rather than perceived problems. Airline regulation was designed to improve safety and increase the overall capacity of the industry by cross-subsidizing travel on low-density routes. Regulation helped set up the safety infrastructure while encouraging the establishment of routes and facilities in smaller cities. Once those tasks were accomplished, there was little need for ongoing regulation, particularly regulation encouraging costly nonprice competition. Economic regulation of the telecommunications industry offers a similar example. Telecommunications regulations were designed to control the natural monopoly aspects of the telecommunications network. However, technological advances such as microwave communications created opportunities for new market entrants. Perhaps one way to distinguish between real and perceived problems is to target only problems associated with measurable costs and benefits. In the case of managed care regulation, efforts should target aspects of managed care organization behavior that can be at least partly attributable to measurable problems in quality or access. Moreover, as Walshe and Shortell argue, "The extent and nature of regulation should be proportionate to the perceived quality problems or need for improvement, in the sense that major problems evoke a major regulatory response, but minor issues receive less regulatory attention."[43]

Third, in cases where regulation appears to be the lowest-cost form of governance, regulations should be designed to take advantage of market incentives within the regulatory umbrella. One of the precursors to deregulation in the electricity sector was the determination that some components of the industry were suitable for regulation (transmission lines), but others were not (generation).[44] Currently, most states employ a hybrid approach to managed care regulation, relying on market-oriented forms of governance, such as selective contracting, to accomplish some of the otherwise regulatory goals. There is a risk, however, that state legislatures will overlook hybrid approaches, as "regulation versus competition" cleavage lines are drawn along party lines.

Fourth, in cases where regulation is likely to be the lowest-cost form of governance, careful attention should be given to the design of regulatory mechanisms.[45] Clearly, any sort of rate or premium regulation is not recommended; the evidence against these forms of regulation is extensive. Similarly, the evidence strongly suggests that creating barriers to market entry is more costly than allowing controlled competition.[46] Provider antitrust exemptions are also ill-advised. If there are sustained structural and behavioral attributes of the industry that consistently favor one economic entity over another, such as health plans over physicians, the resolution of such issues is most appropriately left to the U.S. Department of Justice and the Federal Trade Commission. That leaves a large number of managed care regulatory mechanisms that fall into a gray area of appropriateness. For example, laws allowing health plans to be sued for coverage denials are nominally intended to improve quality by discouraging unwarranted coverage denials. But the mechanism relies on the courts, which are costly both in terms of time and financial resources. Thus, plan liability laws may disproportionately serve those with greater resources. Moreover, large punitive awards are likely to cost health plans nontrivial resources but provide tangible benefits to only a relatively small number of enrollees.

Concluding Remarks

Several aspects of managed care regulation bear resemblance to various forms of economic regulation in other industries. Most managed care regulations are, in theory, intended to reduce uncertainty and information imperfections while creating a level playing field for purchasers, health plans, providers, and enrollees. However, similar to some aspects of economic regulation, many managed care regulations are costly, poorly designed, and of questionable value in terms of benefit. Future debate over managed care regulation should take into consideration four important lessons from economic regulation: The need for regulation should be continually reevaluated; regulations should be aimed at real rather than perceived problems; regulators should seek the optimal mix of regulatory and nonregulatory governance; and regulatory mechanisms should be carefully designed to address problems directly at minimal cost.

5

Competition in Pharmaceutical Markets: The Case of Prescription Drug Marketing

Direct-to-consumer advertising (DTCA) for prescription drugs represents another case where critics contend that the quest for profits results in harm to consumers. For example, Hollon states that "reckoning the cost, economic and otherwise, the public health value of [DTCA] is negligible. Moreover, the effects of [DTCA] are undesirable," mainly because it "undermines the protection that is a result of requiring a physician to certify a patient's need for a prescription drug."[1] Abramson contends that "drug ads usually stay away from the facts that count."[2] The purpose of DTCA, Abramson writes, is not to inform but to create "the impression not only that health and happiness can be achieved by using the right drugs, but that drugs are *necessary* for health and happiness." Further, DTCA is designed to

> evoke a positive emotional connection to the drug, and finally challenge the viewer to . . . discuss the drug with their doctor (in the office, "discuss" usually morphs into "request" or "demand"). . . . [DTCA also] diverts attention from the healthy life habits that usually play a far greater role than advertised drugs in preventing illness and achieving happiness.[3]

Generally, there are two common themes in the case against DTCA for prescription drugs. The first relates to an alleged adverse impact on the clinical quality of care. According to this view, advertising for specific prescription drug products directed toward consumers is at best inherently useless, and at worst often misleading. These advertisements can cause patients harm in the form of unnecessary exposure to risk of adverse events associated with

91

inappropriate and unnecessary drug use. The second complaint relates to what might be termed "economic harm" in the form of resources that are wasted as a result of DTCA. The first and most obvious source of economic waste is a corollary of the proposition that DTCA is useless—if DTCA is indeed useless, then, by definition, any resources devoted to DTCA are wasted. But the greater source of alleged waste relates to excessive use of expensive brand-name drugs resulting from DTCA for these drugs.

At first blush, it is hard to image how providing accurate information about a product to consumers could harm them. Economists have long argued that firms face relatively strong incentives to advertise "search goods"—those goods for which important attributes can be observed prior to purchase.[4] Moreover, firms face strong incentives to engage in truthful advertising of search goods, for two main reasons: First, by definition, the attributes of search goods are observable *ex ante*; and, second, misleading advertising will in most cases harm reputation, thereby in the long run limiting market share to only trial purchases—a result any profit-maximizing firm would find unsustainable.[5] Thus, apart from obvious fraud, abuse, and inappropriate marketing (such as drug ads aimed at minors), economists have more or less dismissed the notion of advertising being harmful and have instead focused on the extent of useful information that may or may not be conveyed.[6]

The case for harm in the case of DCTA for prescription drugs rests on the presumption of "differentness," as discussed in chapter 2. Those who maintain that consumer-directed advertisements for particular drugs are, at best, useless suggest that consumers lack the training, skills, and experience to evaluate the content of DTCA for particular prescription drugs within the context of their specific clinical condition. If physicians and other prescribers already possess this information, then DTCA adds no value. Of course, it is possible that individuals with clinical conditions conducive to treatment with a particular product would not have presented to a physician for treatment in the absence of DTCA. Critics acknowledge that this is a consequence of DTCA, but generally argue that this benefit could be achieved through the use of disease awareness advertisements (those describing a condition without any mention of specific treatments), and that branded DTCA has countervailing adverse effects that outweigh any benefits.

FIGURE 5-1

TREND IN DTCA EXPENDITURES FOR PRESCRIPTION DRUGS,
IN MILLIONS, 2004-EQUIVALENT DOLLARS

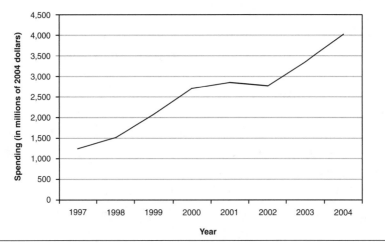

SOURCES: IMS Health (2003; 2006b); U.S. Bureau of Labor Statistics (2006).

In 1997, the Food and Drug Administration (FDA) issued revised regulatory guidance to pharmaceutical manufacturers regarding DTCA, which eased restrictions previously rendering television advertising infeasible.[7] This contributed to an increase in DTCA spending. According to IMS Health data, total DTCA spending rose from $791 million in 1996 to $1.1 billion in 1997, and climbed to $4.0 billion in 2004.[8] As shown in figure 5-1, adjusted for general inflation, the dramatic growth in DTCA expenditure following the revised regulatory guidance stalled from 2000 to 2002, but constant-dollar DTCA spending increased by 20 percent per year from 2002 to 2004. What exactly does all of this DTCA spending do?

Are Prescription Drug Advertisements Misleading?

Advertisements to consumers for prescription drug products must comply with regulatory constraints related to accuracy and "fair balance" imposed by the FDA. The fair balance criterion requires that statements about benefits be balanced with information about risks.[9] At this point, it is worth noting that, in regulating promotional activity directed toward consumers, the FDA uses more stringent requirements for scientific evidence supporting benefit claims than the Federal Trade Commission (FTC), which regulates consumer advertising for nonprescription, "over-the-counter" (OTC) products. Further, although the FTC prohibits deceptive advertising, it does not require fair balance between statements of benefits and risks for OTC products.

The difference in the regulatory constraints on consumer advertising imposed by the FDA and FTC is further amplified by the fact that consumers cannot get access to prescription drugs directly, unlike OTC products. To be able to purchase a prescription drug product, a consumer must find someone legally authorized to write a prescription for it, such as a physician or nurse practitioner. Such health care professionals presumably have access to detailed information from other sources about the product and the potential benefits or risks for use by a particular patient with a particular clinical condition. With this "learned intermediary" sitting between the consumer and use of the advertised prescription drug product, how can an advertisement aimed directly at consumers harm them, even if the advertisement itself is inaccurate or misleading?

But let us assume for the moment that the additional protection for consumers against adverse effects of misleading advertisements afforded by a learned intermediary does not exist. Are prescription drug advertisements often inaccurate and misleading? Even the harshest critics of DTCA for prescription drugs rarely argue that there are any overtly false claims in such advertisements. Rather, in most cases questions about "inaccurate" or "misleading" content relate to the quality of the scientific evidence available to support a benefit claim, or to whether the quantity or quality of risk information is sufficient to provide a fair balance for benefit claims.[10] Thus, prescription drug advertisements that have been labeled "misleading" generally are alleged either to exaggerate benefits or understate risks, or to employ more effective means to communicate clinical benefits than risks, such that risk information is less likely to be understood or retained by the consumer than benefit claims.[11]

Allusions to indirect benefits of treatment are one source of alleged benefit exaggeration.[12] To illustrate the indirect claim issue, consider the case of drugs used to treat type 2 diabetes. It is well established and accepted that the risks of complications of type 2 diabetes (neuropathy, retinopathy, and so forth) are greater over time among persons with higher glycosylated hemoglobin (HbA1c) than among those with lower HbA1c.[13] Thus, it would be reasonable to assume that a drug therapy that improves HbA1c would, at least on average, reduce the risk of these complications of diabetes among patients with lower HbA1c over time. Indeed, this firm belief forms the basis for FDA approval of new drugs for the treatment of type 2 diabetes based on their efficacy in reducing HbA1c. If the FDA used the "reliable and credible" standard for scientific evidence used by the FTC, a manufacturer of such a prescription drug product probably would be permitted to mention in DTCA that use of the product reduces HbA1c, which has been shown to reduce the risks of complications of diabetes. However, the FDA considers any such allusion impermissible in DTCA in which a specific drug is mentioned by name, because the reduced risk of complications was not demonstrated in two large, placebo-controlled, randomized clinical trials *using this specific drug for treatment*. Ironically, conducting any such clinical trials would be unethical, given the strong *a priori* scientific basis for anticipating its outcome. As a result, the drug manufacturer in this case effectively is precluded from *ever* making any such benefit claim in DTCA for the product.

Prescription drug DTCA also has been labeled misleading due to the manner in which benefit and risk information is presented. For example, advertisements for particular drug products typically acknowledge that "results may vary" across individuals, but they do not provide detailed information about the probabilities of treatment responses of different magnitudes. Thus, consumers may overestimate the extent to which use of a particular drug treatment will result in an acceptable improvement in condition in their case. Critics also complain that advertisements for specific brand-name drugs fail to mention that other treatments may provide patients with an equal or even superior improvement in their condition.[14] As a result, consumers may overestimate the benefits and underestimate the risks associated with the use of the advertised prescription drug product. However, consumer surveys indicate that, in general, DTCA increases consumer awareness of both the benefits and risks of prescription drug use, as one might expect, given the fair-balance requirement for DTCA.[15]

In some respects, it is difficult to understand complaints about "inadequate" or "unbalanced" risk information in DTCA in the context of alternative sources of risk information for consumers. Typically, patients receive very little information about prescription drug product risks from physicians or pharmacists.[16] Based on a relatively small, unscientific sample of colleagues in our respective academic institutions, we were unable to identify anyone who could recall ever receiving as much information about the risks associated with the use of a prescription drug via verbal communication with any health care professional as is contained in a typical consumer-directed, sixty-second television advertisement. In this small sample, the risk information provided by health care professionals at the time the drug was prescribed usually related to relatively common—and relatively minor—adverse effects ("Sometimes can cause an upset stomach"), along with suggested steps to manage these effects should they occur. Risks for rare but serious (that is, potentially life-threatening) adverse effects almost never were mentioned. Perhaps our colleagues' experiences are atypical, but more comprehensive surveys (such as those conducted by *Prevention* magazine) confirm that patients who asked their doctors about specific advertised drugs were more likely to receive information about risks for adverse effects than patients who did not ask.[17] This, then, begs the question: Why should "less than ideal" risk information conveyed to consumers via DTCA be considered inferior to the alternative of "almost no" verbal risk information conveyed via health care professionals?[18]

Further, as noted, even if the DTCA for a specific prescription drug misleads consumers, they cannot act on that misinformation and purchase the product without the approval of a health care professional. This learned intermediary typically would be expected to protect consumers from acting on the misleading information. Suppose a DTCA induces a patient who does not have a condition conducive to treatment with the advertised drug to approach a physician to request a prescription for it. In practice, what happens? The following section addresses this question.

Impact of DTCA on Prescriptions

In a recent study, "standardized patients"[19] defined to have either major depression or adjustment disorder with depressive mood were assigned to three groups for each condition: those who requested a specific antidepressant treatment (Paxil) by name; those who requested treatment with an antidepressant but did not ask for a specific drug; and those who made no drug treatment requests.[20] The 298 standardized patients presented to 152 primary care physicians in three cities between May 2003 and May 2004. While consensus and adherence to treatment guidelines are notoriously poor in the case of mental health conditions,[21] current guidelines suggest that treatment with an antidepressant would be considered appropriate for the patients with major depression but would be questionable for those with adjustment disorder.

The results indicated that the standardized patients with major depression who made a general request for antidepressant drug treatment (no brand specified) were most likely to be prescribed antidepressant drug treatment (76 percent), versus those who specifically requested Paxil (53 percent) or made no drug request (31 percent). Among those making a general drug request who received a prescription, few were prescribed Paxil (3 percent), and even among those requesting Paxil who received an antidepressant prescription, only 52 percent were prescribed Paxil. Among standardized patients with adjustment disorder, those who requested Paxil were most likely to receive an antidepressant drug prescription (55 percent), compared to those making a general antidepressant drug request (39 percent) and those making no drug request (10 percent). In further contrast to the results for patients with major depression, among the standardized patients with adjustment disorder who requested Paxil and received an antidepressant drug prescription, 67 percent received Paxil, compared to 26 percent who made a general request and received an antidepressant drug prescription.[22]

Although this study does not address the role of DTCA specifically, it sheds light on the impact of patient requests for specific drugs or drug treatments on the treatments received. Patients with major depression who requested drug treatment were more likely to receive appropriate drug treatment than those who did not. This clearly represents a positive outcome, but requests for drug treatment also resulted in higher rates of antidepressant drug treatment for adjustment disorder. Although the authors interpret this as a negative outcome of patient drug requests, prescribing an antidepressant for such patients is a matter of judgment and is not unambiguously "inappropriate," as indicated by the 10 percent who were given a prescription without asking for one. It is plausible to suggest that some physicians responded to a patient's request for a specific treatment by taking the patient's stated preference into account when selecting among an array of acceptable treatment options. If so, does the resultant greater use of the requested treatment represent a lapse in quality of care caused by DTCA, or is it simply (as discussed in chapter 2) an example of "shared decision-making" among patients and physicians?

But, for the moment, assume that DTCA does induce patients to request prescriptions for Paxil for an unambiguously inappropriate indication, and this in turn results in more inappropriate prescriptions. Does this represent a defect of DTCA? Or does it indicate a deficiency in the quality of mental health service provision in primary care? Among the standardized patients with major depression in the Kravitz study, almost all of those who requested antidepressant treatment received "acceptable" treatment (defined as any combination of antidepressant treatment, mental health referral, or follow-up visit within two weeks)—98 percent among those requesting any antidepressant and 90 percent among those requesting Paxil. But only 56 percent of those making no antidepressant request received acceptable treatment for depression. This finding, coupled with the (possible) overutilization of antidepressants for adjustment disorder, may simply reflect a lack of proficiency among primary care physicians in the diagnosis and treatment of mental health disorders. However, studies focused on other therapeutic areas also find that DTCA results in improvement in the process of care, such as higher rates of appropriate treatment recommendations and enhanced patient adherence.[23]

A somewhat curious result in the Kravitz study is that standardized patients with major depression were less likely to be prescribed *any* antidepressant if they asked for Paxil specifically, versus making a general request for antidepressant treatment. The source of the patient's brand-specific request was not identified in the study, but if the prescribing physicians perceived the request was "caused" by DTCA, this finding is consistent with another recent study focused on physician attitudes about DTCA. Zachry, Dalen, and Jackson found that physician responses to patient requests for specific drugs differed according to the source of information for the request. Specifically, physicians were more likely to report being "annoyed" by the request if it resulted from DTCA, as compared to a request where the patient indicated the drug information was obtained from the *Physician's Desk Reference (PDR)*. Further, physicians were less likely to provide a sample or write a prescription for the requested drug if the request resulted from DTCA versus the *PDR*.[24] Thus, if some of the physicians in the Kravitz study assumed that the brand-specific request resulted from DTCA, this could in part explain the apparent tendency to "punish" drug manufacturers utilizing DTCA by not prescribing Paxil (or any other antidepressant) for patients with major depression who requested Paxil.

Does DTCA have a negative impact on physician-patient interactions? Certainly, the results of several provider surveys suggest many, but not all, physicians dislike DTCA. Virtually all of those surveyed by Robinson and others concluded that DTCA failed to provide adequate information about cost (99 percent) or alternative treatment options (95 percent), and most faulted DTCA for inadequate information about adverse effects (55 percent).[25] Physicians also cited several "problems" caused by DTCA: longer patient encounters (56 percent), requests for specific medications (81 percent), and altered patient expectations about physicians' prescribing behavior (67 percent). Overall, only 43 percent believed DTCA helped their patients become better informed. These results contrast with those from another recent survey of 459 physicians conducted by the FDA.[26] In this survey, 41 percent of physicians believed DTCA had a "somewhat" or "very" positive impact on physician–patient interactions, and 28 percent were neutral, whereas only 5 percent believed the ads had a "very" negative impact. About 17 percent reported that they felt "somewhat" or "very" pressured by their patients to prescribe an advertised drug, and about 18 percent indicated that DTCA had been "a problem" in their interactions with patients.

A common complaint about DTCA in these and other studies of physician attitudes is that the advertisements often forced them to spend time explaining to their patients why drug X "is not right for you" (to paraphrase the ubiquitous closing line in television prescription drug ads). Some might suggest to these physicians that spending time talking to patients is part of their job. But time is money, and physicians could see another patient or go home a little earlier if this expenditure of two or three minutes could be avoided. So some physicians might write a prescription for a drug requested by a patient simply because it takes less time to do so than to explain why an alternative treatment might be more appropriate. This could lead to more extensive use of heavily promoted drugs.

For the sake of argument, take it as a given that DTCA has a profound effect on the way physicians provide medical care to their patients. Does DTCA waste the patient's (or the patient's insurer's) money, or even cause the patient physical harm? We address each of these questions in turn.

Is DTCA Wasteful?

A common complaint about DTCA is that it is a significant contributor to wasteful health spending in the United States. As noted in chapter 1, there are many differences between the U.S. health system and those in other developed countries. Prescription drug DTCA is another potential cause for the alleged excess in U.S. health spending—worldwide, the United States and New Zealand are the only developed countries that permit DTCA for prescription drug products.[27] A recent study funded by health insurers listed the 2000 DTCA spending levels for the most advertised prescription drugs in the U.S. and DTCA spending as a percentage of each drug's U.S. sales (see table 5-1).[28] The report also noted that total 2000 DTCA spending ($2.3 billion) represented about 2.5 percent of total U.S. advertising expenditures for all consumer products that year. These products include Budweiser ($146 million, 3.2 percent of sales), Dell Computers ($160 million, 0.9 percent of sales), and Pepsi ($125 million, 8.9 percent of sales).[29] While these sorts of comparisons tend to make DTCA expenditures appear to be relatively "large," total DTCA spending for prescription drugs was less than 2 percent of total U.S. sales for all brand-name prescription drug products. Further, there is no statistically significant association between the level of DTCA expenditure and the rate of growth in sales for the fifty most advertised brands highlighted in the National Institute for Health Care Management (NIHCM) report.[30]

In any given year, many of the prescription drugs with the highest DTCA spending are relatively new to the U.S. market. As shown in figure 5-2, in 2004 the prescription drug with the highest DTCA spending was Lexapro, with $168 million in DTCA expenditure, representing 10.5 percent of total U.S. Lexapro sales. Lexapro was relatively new to the market in 2004, as were Crestor ($125 million, 21.9 percent of sales) and Bextra

TABLE 5-1

**DTCA EXPENDITURES FOR MOST-ADVERTISED PRESCRIPTION DRUGS
AND SELECTED CONSUMER PRODUCTS, 2000**

Product	DTCA Expenditure (millions of dollars)	Percent of Product Sales
Vioxx	160.8	10.6
Prilosec	107.5	2.6
Claritin	99.7	4.9
Paxil	91.8	5.1
Zocor	91.2	4.1
Viagra	89.5	11.0
Celebrex	78.3	3.9
Flonase	73.5	11.9
Allegra	67.0	6.0
Meridia	65.0	57.4
All Rx Drugs	*2,258.4*	*1.7*
Pepsi	125.0	8.9
Budweiser	146.0	3.2
Dell	160.0	0.9

SOURCES: National Institute for Health Care Management Foundation (2001); author's calculations (see text).

($121 million, 10.1 percent of sales). Similarly, referring back to table 5.1, many of the ten most advertised drugs in 2000 were then relatively new to the market (Vioxx, Viagra, Celebrex, Flonase, and Meridia). Manufacturers with new products are more likely to spend for DTCA to make consumers aware of new treatment options. Most of the other top ten advertised drugs in any given year were at that time facing some type of competitive challenge, such as entry by a new brand-name drug within the same class, or patent expiry of a similar branded drug resulting in within-class generic competition. In 2004, this category included Lipitor, Vioxx, Zoloft, and Nexium. The $114 million in Lipitor DTCA in that year represented 1.6 percent of its $7.1 billion in U.S. sales. Moving beyond the ten most advertised drugs, DTCA spending as percentage of sales generally decreases. For example, DTCA spending for Zithromax, the drug ranked fiftieth in DTCA spending in the

FIGURE 5-2

DTCA EXPENDITURES AND U.S. SALES
FOR THE TEN MOST-ADVERTISED PRESCRIPTION DRUGS IN 2004

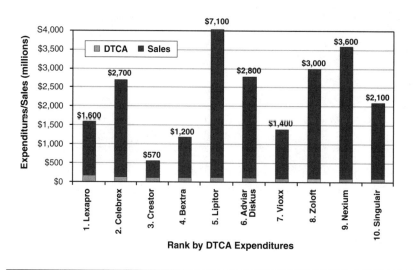

SOURCES: IMS Health (2005b), DTCA spending; NDCHealth (2006), sales.

NIHCM report, was $9.8 million (0.7 percent of sales). Thus, DTCA spending as a percentage of sales is small for most of the hundreds of branded prescription drugs available in the United States with annual sales in excess of $100 million.

If the only source of alleged waste associated with DTCA is spending on advertising by drug manufacturers per se, these data indicate that it would be a relatively trivial contributor to overall spending in the U.S. health care system. But a greater source of concern among critics is the impact of DTCA on patterns of prescription drug use—that is, the inducement of inappropriate use or use of expensive branded drugs in place of equally effective and cheaper drugs.

A claim that inappropriate drug use induced by DTCA is a substantial driver of U.S. health care costs simply lacks face validity. To illustrate, consider that DTCA spending for the ten most advertised drugs listed in table 5-1 accounted for 41 percent of all DTCA drug spending in 2000. In the same year, the cumulative annual sales of these ten most advertised drugs were about $13 billion.[31] Even if as much as 25 percent of the $13 billion in sales for these ten products was for unambiguously inappropriate utilization attributable to DTCA (an implausibly large percentage), the resulting $3.25 billion in "waste" would represent less than 3 percent of the $120.8 billion spent on all prescription drugs in 2000, and less than 0.3 percent of the $1.14 trillion in personal health spending in 2000.[32] In short, given the scale of health care expenditures or even prescription drug expenditures, prescription drug DTCA clearly is too minuscule to be a significant driver of expenditure growth.

Attempts to quantify the impact of DTCA on prescription drug sales are met with daunting methodological challenges.[33] As such, there is no clear consensus in the literature. Indeed, even the pharmaceutical companies themselves are uncertain about their return on investment in DTCA.[34] Several studies conclude that DTCA does contribute to health care cost growth,[35] but the magnitude of the estimated impact varies, and the presumption of causality in observed associations generally is not warranted.[36] Further, existing studies rarely attempt to differentiate DTCA-induced "inappropriate" use from "appropriate" use; they merely attempt to measure the impact on total use. However, many serious conditions conducive to drug treatment are substantially undertreated; increased use of drugs in such cases could reduce other health care costs and improve health outcomes over time.[37] Thus, increases in total drug use are likely to include higher rates of appropriate use, which represent a DTCA-induced improvement in the quality of patient care, not "waste."

Is DTCA Harmful?

Another common complaint about DTCA is that it induces use of highly promoted prescription drugs by patients with little clinical basis for using the products.[38] This not only wastes money, but exposes such patients to risks of drug-related adverse events without a corresponding treatment benefit. A favorite example of those citing harm caused by DTCA in the form of needless exposure to risk is the case of pain-relieving drugs in the class known as cyclooxygenase-2 (COX-2) inhibitors, namely Celebrex (celecoxib), Bextra (valdecoxib), and—especially—Vioxx (rofecoxib).[39]

Sales of Celebrex and Vioxx increased rapidly after their introduction into the U.S. market in 1999.[40] At the same time, these prescription drugs also were among the most heavily promoted in terms of DTCA. In 2000, spending on DTCA for Vioxx in the U.S. was $161 million, more than any other prescription drug, and DTCA spending on Celebrex was $78 million, ranking it seventh in DTCA spending.[41] In the same year, U.S. sales totaled $2.0 billion for Celebrex and $1.5 billion for Vioxx. However, the growth in sales subsequently tapered off—in 2003, U.S. sales totaled $2.6 billion for Celebrex and $1.8 billion for Vioxx.[42] In that same year, the cost of Vioxx ($75 per month) or Celebrex ($110 per month)[43] exceeded by several orders of magnitude the monthly cost for alternative treatments available over the counter as inexpensive generics, mainly "nonspecific nonsteroidal anti-inflammatory drugs" (nonspecific NSAIDs) such as ibuprofen (Advil) and naproxen (Aleve).

Pointing to the lack of superior pain relief efficacy for COX-2s versus nonspecific NSAIDs, critics complained that the growth in COX-2 sales must have been driven by massive DTCA spending; since the COX-2 drugs offered "little benefit" over nonspecific NSAIDs for most patients, there was little clinical rationale for their use. By this argument, DTCA led to overuse of these new and expensive drugs, resulting in excessive cost. Moreover, as emerging safety concerns led Merck, the manufacturer of Vioxx, to withdraw it voluntarily from the market, critics charged that DTCA caused consumers harm by exposing them to needless risk through inappropriate DTCA-induced use of COX-2 inhibitors. We focus on the Vioxx episode as a case study to address the more general charge that DTCA for prescription drugs causes harm to consumers.

Case Study: Vioxx

First, some background information about the clinical challenge motivating the development of COX-2 inhibitors will help to establish the context for the case. Chronic pain, such as pain from osteoarthritis and rheumatoid arthritis, generally is treated with some form of NSAID, a broad class that includes COX-2 inhibitors and many nonspecific NSAIDs, such as ibuprofen and naproxen, and the original NSAID—aspirin. Nonspecific or nonselective

NSAIDs are so labeled because they inhibit both the COX-1 and COX-2 enzymes. The COX-2 enzyme reinforces inflammation that causes pain, while the COX-1 enzyme protects the stomach and the gastrointestinal system.[44] Thus, the concept behind the development of the COX-2 inhibitors was to find drugs that would specifically or selectively inhibit COX-2 but not inhibit COX-1, thereby (at least in theory) avoiding the adverse effects of COX-1 inhibition associated with the use of nonspecific NSAIDs.

These adverse effects of nonspecific NSAIDs are not the mere occurrence of the occasionally upset tummy. The ongoing use of nonspecific NSAIDs in doses commonly used for chronic pain can result in life-threatening gastrointestinal bleeding. Specifically, the attributable risk of death from gastrointestinal adverse effects associated with the use of nonspecific NSAIDs for two months or more in doses sufficient to achieve arthritis pain relief has been estimated to be 1 in 1,200.[45] While this risk may seem low enough, given the large number of patients using these drugs, Wolfe and colleagues conclude that these drug-induced gastrointestinal deaths, if tabulated separately in the U.S. vital statistics, would be the fifteenth most common cause of death in the United States.[46] Thus, patients in severe chronic pain often have had to make difficult decisions, trading off relief from pain and the often unpleasant and sometimes fatal adverse effects of nonspecific NSAIDs.[47]

In clinical trials focused on pain relief, patients taking COX-2 inhibitors generally achieved pain relief similar to what could be achieved using nonspecific NSAIDs. As noted, critics often cite this result as proof that COX-2 inhibitors are no more "efficacious" than older nonspecific NSAIDs. But the purported benefit of COX-2 inhibitors over the older pain drugs was a lower incidence of gastrointestinal adverse effects, not clearly superior pain relief. Clinical trials focused on pain relief supported the conclusion that rates of gastrointestinal adverse events were less common among users of COX-2 inhibitors compared to users of nonspecific NSAIDs.[48] Further, in usual practice, many patients cannot tolerate the high doses of nonspecific NSAIDs used in clinical trials. Thus, the level of pain relief achieved in usual clinical practice using a COX-2 inhibitor may be greater than the level of relief attainable using nonspecific NSAIDs.[49] Indeed, in usual practice, patients taking a COX-2 for chronic pain were less likely to discontinue therapy or switch pain medications compared to those taking nonspecific NSAIDs,[50] presumably due in part to a lower rate of gastrointestinal adverse effects or superior ease of use (for example, less frequent dosing). Thus, in usual clinical practice, treatment of chronic pain with COX-2s could be more effective and entail lower risk of serious gastrointestinal adverse events than treatment using a nonspecific NSAID.

However, as more data about COX-2 inhibitors accumulated, a potential risk for cardiovascular adverse events emerged as a safety question. In a clinical trial focused on treatment for arthritis pain, patients treated with Vioxx had a lower rate of gastrointestinal adverse effects compared to patients treated with naproxen, but they also had a higher rate of cardiovascular adverse events.[51] One particular NSAID (aspirin) previously had been shown to reduce the risk of cardiovascular events in clinical trials. Although such large-scale trials were lacking for other nonspecific NSAIDs, including naproxen, one possible explanation was that naproxen reduced cardiovascular risk, in a manner similar to aspirin.[52] Thus, the interpretation of the cardiovascular risk differential in the trial was ambiguous—did Vioxx increase the risk for cardiovascular events, or did naproxen reduce the risk?

A partial answer to this question was provided through a subsequent placebo-controlled clinical trial focusing on Vioxx as a treatment to prevent colon cancer. The trial was halted in September 2004 (shortly before it was scheduled to end) as it became clear that there were more serious cardiovascular events among patients treated with Vioxx compared to placebo.[53] Merck, the manufacturer of Vioxx, decided to withdraw the product voluntarily from all markets worldwide—they did not consult with the FDA prior to making this decision.[54] In a subsequent review of all available data for NSAIDs, the FDA concluded that all COX-2 inhibitors were associated with an increased risk of cardiovascular disease events, that available data did not permit any conclusions about a ranking of this risk within the COX-2 class, and that existing studies "[did] not clearly demonstrate" that this risk was greater for COX-2s than for other NSAIDs, in large part due to a lack of data concerning the cardiovascular safety of the latter.[55] Indeed, in February 2005 an FDA advisory panel voted (albeit by a slim 17–15 majority) to permit Vioxx to reenter the U.S. market—although Merck thus far has not attempted to reintroduce the product.[56] Two recent reviews essentially affirm the FDA's conclusions.[57] Specifically, Kearney and colleagues find no differences in cardiovascular risks among COX-2s, and conclude that cardiovascular risks for high doses of commonly used older NSAIDs overall are similar to the risks for COX-2s, though these risks may be lower for a specific NSAID (naproxen).

The Vioxx episode brings to mind a quote from a now-classic paper by Sir Austin Bradford Hill on the role of scientific information in guiding policy decisions:

> All scientific work is incomplete—whether it be observational or experimental. All scientific work is liable to be upset or modified by advancing knowledge. That does not confer upon us a freedom to ignore the knowledge we already have, or to postpone the action that it appears to demand at a given time.[58]

One might think that Merck would be commended for conducting a trial to collect the data needed to better assess the cardiovascular effects of its product (data that are not available for most NSAIDs), and for its decisive action to withdraw Vioxx on its own initiative as new data about the product emerged.[59] The company could have waited to see what action the FDA might take, or stalled making a decision pending additional data. Of course, Merck has not been commended; it has been vilified and subjected to numerous product liability lawsuits.[60] Perhaps this episode merely confirms a commonly evoked, sardonic variant of an old aphorism: "No good deed goes unpunished."

With this background information in mind, the charge that DTCA for Vioxx harmed consumers rests on the proposition that a substantial portion of the growth in Vioxx sales is attributable to DTCA, causing some specific patients to use Vioxx when treatment with a nonspecific NSAID could have been appropriate (namely, patients at low risk for bleeding).[61] However, as noted, it is difficult to establish the impact of DTCA for a particular drug product on its sales, let alone its impact on "inappropriate" use. Though relatively high rates of DTCA for COX-2s corresponded to strong sales growth after the products were introduced in the United States, the case for causality in this association is weakened by the fact that similarly strong rates of take-up following the introduction of COX-2s were observed in other developed countries where DTCA is prohibited.[62]

Further, while some NSAIDs are "contraindicated" (should never be used) for patients with a history of gastrointestinal bleeding, all NSAIDs increase the risk of gastrointestinal bleeding, even among those with no such history. However, the risk of gastrointestinal adverse effects is lower for COX-2s compared to nonspecific NSAIDs. Thus, while it might be reasonable to conclude that patients at high risk for bleeding should not use some NSAIDs, it is a value judgment to contend that those at low risk should not use COX-2s. Of course, the issue of uncertainty about the cardiovascular risks of NSAIDs complicates the picture. Once again, patients with chronic pain have to make a difficult trade-off between relief from pain and gastrointestinal and cardiovascular risks. Given the uncertainty, such decisions must be based on the best data available at the time patients have to choose their treatment. Patients with different levels of (or tolerance for) pain, and different preferences over risks, will have different preferences for treatments.

But, for the sake of argument, suppose misleading DTCA for COX-2 drugs caused patients to believe these drugs offered more effective pain relief than older NSAIDs, which in turn led patients to ask physicians to prescribe a COX-2. Physicians might accede to this request as long as they believed a COX-2 would be "no worse" for the patient than an older NSAID. That one treatment has a higher cost than the other has little or no practical relevance for physicians under prevailing patterns of physician compensation.

Of course, the cost of alternative treatments should matter to the buyer. But in the presence of health insurance, the patient does not have to pay all of the difference in costs between alternative treatments. Doshi and others found that COX-2 drugs were more commonly used than nonspecific NSAIDs among elderly patients at greater risk for gastrointestinal adverse effects, as one would expect, but the difference became smaller with the generosity of prescription drug insurance.[63] In other words, patients who had to pay most of the additional costs themselves were less likely to use a COX-2 drug when they had less "need" for a COX-2 than those who paid very little of the additional cost. Thus, any harm from excessive use of COX-2 drugs resulting from DTCA came, in part, from a lack of an incentive among physicians and patients to consider value in making treatment choices.

DTCA Regulation

The preceding discussion suggests there is little evidence to indicate that DTCA is a substantive contributor to excess health spending, or that it generally causes harm for patients. But suppose DTCA (and other promotional activity by pharmaceutical companies) in at least some cases induces patients to make ill-advised requests for treatments, and causes physicians to offer drug treatments contrary to their patients' best interests—why not just ban these activities? After all, DTCA for prescription drugs is banned in almost all developed nations.[64] However, in the United States there are constitutional protections for speech, even (to a degree) commercial speech. The current "Central Hudson" criteria for the extent of permissible governmental restrictions relate to the following considerations:[65]

- Is the expression protected (that is, "pure" speech)?

- Is the asserted governmental interest in regulation substantial?

- Does the regulation directly advance the governmental interest?

- Is the regulation more extensive than necessary to advance the governmental interest?

Permissible restrictions must satisfy the first and fourth conditions in the negative and the middle two conditions in the affirmative.

While the government can (and does) regulate the content of DTCA as well as promotion to physicians (for example, "detail" visits by pharmaceutical sales representatives), it would be difficult to regulate the frequency of these activities, or ban them altogether. Indeed, recent court decisions have affirmed that some regulatory efforts to curtail the promotion of tobacco products were too restrictive.[66] It certainly is easier to make the case for "harm" associated with tobacco promotion than the promotion of prescription drugs.

Although the issue of permissible limits on DTCA for prescription drugs remains unresolved, [67] even critics concede that a broad prohibition on DTCA for all prescription drugs would be considered "more extensive than necessary" to advance the governmental interest.[68] The FDA does ban "reminder" advertisements for certain drugs deemed to entail substantial safety risks (those with "black box" safety warnings). Reminder advertisements simply mention the drug by name but do not mention a treatment indication, nor do they provide any risk information. The FDA does not permit such advertisements because it requires all promotional materials for these high-risk drugs to include risk information.[69] The restrictive DTCA regulations for black box drugs are directionally consistent with a greater potential for significant harm associated with inappropriate use as compared to other prescription drugs. Such restrictions may not be needed to protect the public from potential harm, but the fact that DTCA currently is permitted even for high-risk drugs indicates that extreme restrictions for less risky drugs probably would be judged to be unreasonable.

Even if DTCA for prescription drugs could be prohibited, would it be good public policy? Probably not. In general, the literature suggests that information disseminated to consumers improves the functioning of markets and enhances consumer welfare.[70] The case against DTCA for prescription drugs rests on the "differentness" assumption, as discussed in chapter 2. However, the most salient difference between prescription drugs and consumer products is the wedge between the product's price and what consumers pay, created by health insurance. Thus, it would be more appropriate to attribute any excess utilization of prescription drugs associated with DTCA to moral hazard rather than DTCA per se.

Manufacturers of brand-name prescription drugs have the incentive to devote resources to advertising their products. Accurate information about prescription drugs disseminated through advertising and other promotional activity may enhance the quality of care. Physicians tend to adhere to evidence-based treatment guidelines relating to the use of pharmaceuticals in treatment more than they do to recommendations in guidelines relating to other aspects of treatment for which no commercial promotion occurs.[71] Further, as noted, DTCA appears to enhance patient adherence to drug therapy to a greater degree than promotion directed toward physicians only.[72]

Concluding Remarks

There is little evidence that DTCA for prescription drugs is a significant source of growth in health care costs, or that it commonly causes physical harm to consumers. Indeed, it is more likely to be the case that current regulatory policy concerning DTCA for prescription drugs harms consumers by unduly restricting the dissemination of accurate information that might empower them to make better value assessments. DTCA increases the awareness of information about the benefits of treatment as well as the risks, directly through the advertisements themselves and by motivating consumers to seek additional information from other sources.[73] This enhanced information contributes to greater use of appropriate drug treatments among the previously untreated, and better adherence to therapy among those receiving treatment.

Even if DTCA creates waste or causes harm in some instances, banning advertising treats the symptoms rather than the disease. In an ideal world, a physician would endeavor to compare the incremental costs and benefits of alternative treatments, using lower-cost generic drugs whenever the incremental cost of a branded drug exceeded its incremental benefits. In other words, a physician would help solve what Dranove labels the patient's "shopping problem."[74] But physicians are not compensated according to how well they solve the patient's shopping problem. In a fee-for-service practice, they are paid to conduct activities such as patient visits. Even physicians in salaried practices have productivity quotas to satisfy. It takes a physician no more time to write a prescription for an expensive brand-name drug promoted using DTCA when a patient requests the drug by name than to explain how to use an equally acceptable and inexpensive over-the-counter treatment alternative. Indeed, writing the prescription may take less time. If the physician expects the patient to achieve a similar clinical outcome in either case, under current compensation arrangements he or she has no particular reason to favor one treatment over the other. The fact that one means to the desired end costs a lot more than the other is not the physician's problem.

One way to make it the physician's problem is to devise mechanisms of compensation that provide financial rewards to physicians who do a good job of solving the patient's shopping problem. But that is easier said than done. Capitation (a fixed payment per patient per period of time) provides an incentive to use cheaper means to produce similar outcomes. But it also can provide an incentive to use cheaper means to achieve inferior outcomes. To avoid the latter undesirable result requires a robustly competitive market for capitation contracts—those physicians who choose to produce poor care will be at risk of losing contracts. This, in turn, requires reliable mechanisms to measure and credible means of communicating information about the quality of care provided. The development of independent third-party "quality scorecards" for providers represents a movement in this direction.

In general, health system reforms that seek to make consumers better "value" shoppers for health care services are needed. The managed care model made use of agency relationships to make value assessments on the behalf of health plan members. The development of consumer-directed health care represents a movement toward assigning this responsibility directly to consumers. Under this system, consumers have powerful incentives to consider value when making drug purchases, but they must have access to accurate information to make such decisions. Effectively functioning markets require informed participants, and policies designed to enhance the dissemination of drug information to consumers are more likely to be beneficial to consumers than public policies restricting their access to information.

Conclusions and Policy Implications

Some common themes emerge from the preceding chapters. First and foremost, there is no doubt that there is ample room for improvement in the U.S. health care system. Given the well-documented positive effects of insurance on health, insuring the uninsured should remain a top state and federal policy objective. But there is no consensus about how to improve access; proposed solutions span the spectrum of administrative controls versus market incentives, from a single-payer government insurance system to mandated employer health benefits to consumer-directed, defined-contribution health spending accounts. Proponents of sweeping reforms often point to health systems in other developed nations as models to be emulated. However, as we have argued, comparison countries have many shortcomings, and it is not at all clear whether the benefits of centralized control would offset the costs of a centralized system were it to be implemented in the United States. Most health systems in other developed nations face unsustainable growth in spending and, in some cases, increasingly intolerable lapses in functional access. The same dynamic forces of population demographics and technological advances apply in these systems as well.

The balance of evidence suggests that markets have much to offer, and the unencumbered functioning of health care markets has largely been untested in the United States. Many of the aspects of health care that make it seem unique are observed in other complex services and goods, many of which are organized with markets and prices as the primary means of resource allocation. A variety of institutions and organizational forms has evolved to enable markets for such products to function effectively, despite their complexity. Within the context of these institutions and organizational forms, the available evidence suggests that competition in health care spurs innovation, induces efficiency, and enhances quality, just as it does in other types of markets and industries. But to reap the potential benefits of competition, policymakers need to move beyond knee-jerk discomfort with the mechanisms of markets. For example, as we discussed in the preceding chapter, and as has been argued for quite some time by economists, advertising conveys some useful information to consumers.[1]

As an example of the likely harms of too much market interference, the case of specialty hospitals is apposite. There appear to be distinct economic advantages associated with specialization, due mainly to process improvement, learning, avoidance of diseconomies of scope, and focus on core competencies. Specialty hospitals appear to have equal or better patient outcomes compared to their general-hospital counterparts. Hence, there is no evidence to suggest that specialty hospitals should be barred from entering acute inpatient care markets on the basis of efficiency or quality of care. Moreover, specialty hospitals compete with general hospitals in the same manner in which general hospitals compete with each other. We found that profit margins of general hospitals have certainly not been hurt by the entry of specialty hospitals. In addition, there is no evidence that physician self-referral is a problem in specialty hospitals. Physician self-referral is likely to play a relatively minor role in patient utilization of specialty hospitals, because physicians' ownership interests tend to be small; and the associated financial incentive to use the specialty hospital is small and indirect relative to the larger and more direct financial incentive from the professional fee for providing the service itself.

At least two of the reform initiatives that have surfaced recently—managed care regulation and California's single-payer health plan—rely extensively on regulatory mechanisms that have been shown to result in inefficiencies and higher prices in other industries. For example, several aspects of managed care regulation bear resemblance to various forms of economic regulation in other industries. Most managed care regulations are, in theory, intended to reduce uncertainty and information imperfections while creating a level playing field for purchasers, health plans, providers, and enrollees. However, similar to some aspects of economic regulation, many managed care regulations are costly, poorly designed, and of questionable value in terms of benefit.

Some Policy Implications

The solution to this conundrum is not immediately obvious; perhaps if it were, some coordinated version of health reform would have been implemented when the opportunities presented themselves, such as during the debates over the 1994 Clinton health plan. One way to approach the problem, however, is to consider the extremes of the continuum: On one end is a predominantly private system, with most of the incentives of competition and free enterprise largely intact, and on the other end is a single governmental administrator and payer, similar to the Canadian system.

There are a number of ways in which to organize economic activity, the most prevalent examples of which include free markets, regulated markets, hierarchical organizations, and government organizations (that is, public administration or public governance). No form of organization is per se superior; each has its merits, and each is designed to facilitate specific kinds of transactions.[2] A critical component of the assessment of a centralized government health care system is to identify the comparative strengths and weaknesses of public versus private governance. Public governance seems to work well for defense, parks, police and safety, and the like. But apart from those familiar examples of public goods and services, there are many goods and services for which the public versus private question is largely unresolved, such as utilities, education, prisons, and even armed services.

We can address the same problem by asking the question: Why does the United States rely on a hybrid, mixed-market government model to deliver health care? The usual answers to that question, as we have suggested in the preceding chapters, typically involve concepts like path dependency, weak political property rights, lack of leadership, and so on— the implication being that the existing system is suboptimal, and that a superior alternative exists.

But in theory and in practice, in health and nonhealth industries, dominant organizational designs tend to be the end result of experimentation, evaluation, and selection, much like the phylogenetic development of species over time.[3] Attempts by policymakers in the United States to achieve anything other than incremental changes to the health care system closely follow a classic dominant design story: "As an organization gains experience and, thereby, proficiency with the current activities, procedures, or technologies," writes Levinthal, "it becomes less likely that experimentation with alternatives will appear attractive or, if attempted, prove desirable." Radical changes, on the other hand, are observed primarily in cases of "sustained poor performance" on the part of the organization.[4] Although there are many who would argue that the U.S. system has performed poorly in past years, the main objective of chapter 1 was to argue that its performance is at least as good as those of other developed countries, even those with national single-payer systems.

Thus, from this perspective, hybrid health care systems are not so much a compromise as perhaps an optimal solution to the coordinated versus autonomous adaptation problem. Rather than focus on the endpoints—free enterprise on one end and government control on the other—a potentially better alternative would be to work toward optimizing the extant hybrid system. The primary challenge of a hybrid system is deciding which components are suitable for market competition and which are appropriate candidates for government control. While the hybrid system might, as a whole, represent a dominant design, it is unlikely that the allocation of market forces within the system's architecture is optimal.

As we have argued throughout this book, some aspects of the hybrid system appear to be working quite well; the best evidence for this is that the United States is an international leader in many aspects of health care quality, innovation, and organization. Although many areas need attention, we believe five might be considered the best places to start:

The Reduction, Revision, or Elimination of Laws and Regulations that Inhibit the Functioning of Markets. First and perhaps foremost, as many other economists have argued, markets should be allowed to work in the cases where we know they work well. In order to harness markets' full potential, public policies and regulation must be crafted in such a way as to permit them to work within the larger policy structure. We might think of this strategy as one of "embedded" markets; for example, a "macro" health policy objective might be to extend health care benefits to all U.S. residents, but the tools to accomplish that end might include relying on markets for the delivery of many of the components of coverage. Many existing regulations, such as CON and certain kinds of managed care regulations, inhibit the functioning of embedded markets. Many broad-brush solutions, such as California's proposed single-payer plan, throw the baby out with the bathwater by proposing to eliminate market forces wherever possible.

The Development of a More Coherent Strategy to Evaluate New Medical Technologies and Services. Economic evaluation of health care processes and technologies does not necessarily have to be something that only national health systems care about. As Pauly has recently argued, "It is the reduction of the anxiety associated with this vagueness about value, rather than guaranteed improvements in quality and efficiency, that would be the biggest dividend of a transparently competitive health care market."[5]

The Infusion of Transparency into the Making of Contracts between Health Plans and Enrollees. A large number of problems observed in the relationship between enrollees and their health plans might be addressed through more transparent and explicit contracting.[6] Havighurst submits that, "to the greatest extent possible, the nature, intensity, and content of the services provided under competing health plans should be established in health plan contracts."[7] The application of innovative contracts, particularly "relational" contracts, has been increasingly relied upon in other industries where transactions are considered relatively complex.[8]

The Redesigning of Health Insurance to Imbue a Greater Degree of Price Sensitivity within Health Services Transactions. The growing popularity of high-deductible health plans, whether coupled with health savings accounts or not, offers a promising vehicle through which to introduce greater price sensitivity in health care markets.[9] In response to enrollee demand, some health plans have recently undertaken efforts to supply their customers with provider price information.[10] High-deductible plans should ideally be designed to eliminate excess utilization (the "bad" moral hazard) while promoting the consumption of proven preventive services (the "good" moral hazard).[11]

Improved Marketing and Coordination among Existing Public Insurance Programs. Market forces can help control cost inflation, which may in turn make health insurance more affordable to more people. But cost control alone is not sufficient to extend coverage to all those who currently

are uninsured. For this group, there are many existing government programs. These include, but are not limited to, Medicaid, the Children's Health
Insurance Program (CHIP; also given state-specific names, like Healthy Families in California), county-sponsored programs, programs for immigrants
awaiting legal status, programs for pregnant women and infants, and other
county-level programs for low-income residents. Many of these programs are
undersubscribed, for a variety of reasons. In some cases, programs are at
only 50 percent of capacity. For example, several years ago California had to
return hundreds of millions of dollars of unused federal CHIP funds. One
reason is insufficient marketing and outreach on the part of the program's
sponsors. Another is lack of coordination between program administrators
and points of access, such as schools and other state and local assistance programs. Efforts should be made to improve the coordination, marketing, and
outreach of these programs.

These five points represent areas in which policymakers, business leaders, and health industry leaders might best focus their attention. Too often,
business and policy solutions are perceived as either black or white, or in
terms of "us versus them"; examples include debates over replacing the current system with a Canadian-style, single-payer system at one end of the
spectrum, to relying solely on markets at the other. Rather than occupying
extreme endpoints, health care delivery in the United States is more likely
to be made up of a collection of programs, products, regulations, and markets. Each one of these elements has something to offer. The key to improving health care delivery lies in striking a balance that maximizes all of the
benefits of markets and consumer choice while using the most appropriate
and efficient government instruments to extend access to care to those who
want it but cannot afford it.

Notes

Introduction

1. World Health Organization (2000).
2. Docteur, Suppanz, and Woo (2003).
3. Mueller (2001, 4).
4. Bartlett and Steele (2004).
5. Kassirer (2004).
6. Abramson (2005, 242–53).
7. Kleinke (2001, 6, 21, 45).
8. Mueller (2001, 194); Bartlett and Steele (2004, ch. 6).
9. Cutler (2004); Dranove (2000); Robinson (1999); Herzlinger (1997; 2004a); Cannon and Tanner (2005).
10. U.S. Federal Trade Commission and U.S. Department of Justice (2004).

Chapter 1: U.S. Health System Performance: An International Perspective

1. A purchasing power parity (PPP) index is a cross-sectional price index that summarizes differences in prevailing prices for a common set of goods and services within different countries. A PPP is conceptually analogous to an intertemporal price index, such as the Consumer Price Index (CPI), which summarizes differences in prices within a country at different points in time.

2. Recent dramatic increases in oil prices have induced a spike in per-capita GDP in small, oil-rich Norway. According to the most recent data (OECD 2006), in 2004, PPP-adjusted GDP per capita in Norway ($38,800) was almost equal to GDP per capita in the United States ($39,700).

3. Docteur, Suppanz, and Woo (2003).

4. For Poland, Sweden, and Turkey, 1999 data are used in the regression analysis because data for 2000 are not available.

5. The predicted value of "log of health spending per capita" was transformed from log-dollars into dollars using a nonparametric smearing estimator (see Duan 1983).

6. Note that the estimated residual for Turkey, at the opposite extreme from the United States in the OECD sample distribution, also is somewhat sensitive to the shape specification in the regression model.

7. As noted, rapid increases in oil prices have resulted in sharp increases in per-capita GDP for Norway, but these have not been matched by contemporaneously sharp increases in health spending. Thus, regression models fitted to recent samples with higher GDP for Norway generally result in larger U.S. residuals.

8. See, for example, Blendon et al. (2002).

9. Levi et al. (2002); Morse (2002).

10. Aoki (1990).

11. Kaiser Family Foundation (2004a).

12. Anderson et al. (2003).

13. Fuchs and Hahn (1990).

14. Danzon (1999); Danzon and Chao (2000); Berndt (2000).

15. U.S. Department of Commerce. International Trade Administration (2004).

16. Morrisey (1994).

17. Schneider and Pope (1992); Nicholson (2002).

18. Woolhandler, Campbell, and Himmelstein (2003).

19. Robinson (1997); Aaron (2003).

20. See, for example, Woolhandler and Himmelstein (1997).

21. Robinson (1997). The role of managerial and administrative functions in enabling organizations to achieve their objectives has been broadly studied. Chester Barnard's *The Functions of the Executive* (1964) is considered one of the cornerstone works on this topic. Oliver Williamson and others provide similar but more recent perspectives (Milgrom and Roberts 1992; Williamson 1991; 1996).

22. Danzon (1992).

23. The queuing issue is exacerbated by moral hazard, whereby consumers behave differently when they have insurance. Behavioral changes associated with moral hazard include changes in health behaviors (for example, smoking more), but also in the levels of consumption of medical services (for example, consuming more services than otherwise would have been consumed in the absence of insurance).

24. Kahn et al. (2005).

25. See, for example, Studdert et al. (2005).

26. Kessler and McClellan (1996).

27. U.S. Department of Health and Human Services. Office of the Assistant Secretary for Planning and Evaluation (2003).

28. Anderson et al. (2005).

29. Morrisey, Kilgore, and Nelson (2006).

30. Danzon (2000).

31. See, for example, Danzon and Chao (2000).

32. U.S. Department of Health and Human Services. Centers for Disease Control. National Center for Health Statistics (2002a).

33. U.S. Department of Health and Human Services. Centers for Disease Control. National Center for Health Statistics (2002b).

34. U.S. Department of Health and Human Services. Centers for Disease Control. National Center for Health Statistics (2002a).

35. In contrast, the suicide rate in the United States is below the OECD mean. More importantly in the context of our discussion, suicide rates, unlike homicide, may reflect health system performance, since suicide often is a consequence of potentially treatable mental illness (Hussey et al. 2004).

36. Ibid.

37. Ibid., 91–92.

38. Miller and Frech (2004, 14–15).

39. Body-mass index is calculated as weight (in kilograms) divided by the square of height (in meters).

40. McGinnis and Foege (1993).

41. Sturm (2002).

42. Miller and Frech (2004, chapter 5).

43. Ibid.

44. Goldstein et al. (2005); Weber et al. (2005); Guendelman et al. (2006).

45. Asch et al. (2006).

46. Hadley and Reschovsky (2002); Schoen et al. (2005a).

47. Schoen et al. (2005a). The definition of underinsured is based on cost-exposure to family income. The underinsured were defined as those with at least one of three indicators: (1) out-of-pocket medical expenses greater than or equal to 10 percent of income; (2) out-of-pocket medical expenses greater than or equal to 5 percent of income if income is less than 200 percent of the federal poverty level; and (3) health plan deductibles greater than or equal to 5 percent of income.

48. Kronick and Gilmer (1999).

49. U.S. Bureau of the Census (2005a, table H101).

50. U.S. Congress. Congressional Budget Office (2003); Kaiser Family Foundation (2004b); American Enterprise Institute (2005).

51. Strunk and Reschovsky (2002).

52. Copeland (1998); U.S. Congress. Congressional Budget Office (2003).

53. Schoen et al. (2005a).

54. Berger et al. (1999).

55. Short (2000).

56. Economic Research Initiative on the Uninsured (2005).

57. Kaiser Family Foundation (2004b).

58. Pauly and Nichols (2004); Schur, Feldman, and Zhao (2004).

59. Jensen and Morrisey (1999).

60. Fuhrmans (2005).

61. Davidoff, Garrett, and Yemane (2001).

62. Klerman, Ringel, and Roth (2005); Peterson and Grady (2005).

63. Klerman et al. (2005), 12.
64. Peterson and Grady (2005), 11.
65. Bell et al. (1999).
66. Schoen et al. (2005b, 519).
67. Blendon et al. (2002, 188).
68. Alter et al. (1999).
69. Naylor et al. (1990).
70. Hemingway et al. (2000).
71. Arnesen, Erikssen, and Stavem (2002); Hughes and Griffiths (1997); Naylor and Levinton (1993); Naylor et al. (1992); Naylor et al. (1993).
72. Naylor et al. (1995); Llewellyn-Thomas et al. (1999).
73. Bishai and Lang (2000).
74. *Chaoulli v. Quebec* 1 S. C. R. 791 at para. 123, 2005 SCC 35.

Chapter 2: Is Profit-Seeking Inappropriate in Health Care?

1. Robinson (2001, 1045).
2. See, for example, Relman and Reinhardt (1986) and Rice (1998).
3. Robinson (2001).
4. As an example, see http://www.walmartmovie.com for the documentary "Wal-Mart: The High Cost of Low Price" (Greenwald 2005).
5. See, for example, Rice (1998).
6. Arrow (1963).
7. Rosenberg (1987).
8. 42 U.S.C., § 291.
9. See, for example, Harris (1977).
10. Sloan et al. (2001); Shen et al. (2005).
11. Vita and Sacher (2001).
12. Horwitz (2005).
13. Mobley and Bradford (1997).
14. Panel on the Nonprofit Sector (2005); Illinois Attorney General (2006).
15. Kane and Wubbenhorst (2000).
16. Appleby (2004).
17. Dranove, Shanley, and Simon (1992).
18. Havighurst (1974); Salkever and Bice (1979).
19. Sloan (1988); Antel, Ohsfeldt, and Becker (1995).
20. Conover and Sloan (1998); Grabowski, Ohsfeldt, and Morrisey (2003).
21. Conover and Sloan (1998, 476–77).
22. Salkever and Bice (1979); Sloan (1988); Antel, Ohsfeldt, and Becker (1995).
23. U.S. Federal Trade Commission and U.S. Department of Justice (2004, 22).
24. Halm, Lee, and Chassin (2002).
25. Vaughan-Sarrazin et al. (2002).

26. Bernstein (1972); U.S. Federal Trade Commission and U.S. Department of Justice (2004). As an extreme example, consider the case of former Alabama governor Don Siegelman and former HealthSouth CEO Richard Scrushy. An indictment charges that the latter bribed the former to secure the chairmanship of the Alabama CON review board (United States Attorney's Office Middle District of Alabama, December 20, 2005). Abstracting from the bribery charges, the fact that a sitting hospital CEO was in the position to influence judgments of the "need" for entry by potential competitors speaks for itself.

27. Chernew, Gowrisankaran, and Fendrick (2002).

28. Leapfrog Group (2006).

29. Ohsfeldt et al. (1998).

30. *Kentucky Association of Health Plans Inc. v. Miller*, 123 S.Ct. 1471 (2003).

31. See, for example, Demsetz (1967); Furubotn and Pejovich (1972); De Alessi (1983); Hart (1995); Hansmann (1996); Furubotn and Richter (1997).

32. See, for example, Boardman and Vining (1989).

33. Kessler and McClellan (2000, 610).

34. Kessler and McClellan (2002).

35. Kessler and Geppert (2005).

36. Santerre and Vernon (2005, 15).

37. Grabowski and Hirth (2003).

38. Devereaux, Choi, et al. (2002); Devereaux, Schunemann, et al. (2002, 2456).

39. Brooks et al. (2006).

40. Bodenheimer (2003).

41. According to Health Care for All—California (2005), the leading reported feature of the bill is that "everyone is covered. No one will ever lose coverage for any reason."

42. The 2005 proposed California Health Insurance Reliability Act would confer substantial powers on the elected health insurance commissioner; for instance, "These broad powers shall include, but are not limited to, the power . . . to set rates; to establish [CHIS] goals, standards and priorities; . . . [and to] make allocations and reallocations to the health planning regions and promulgate generally binding regulations concerning any and all matters related to the implementation of the division and its purposes" (§140101 [b] 25–33).

43. Refer to SB 840 §140500–§140502 for a list of covered benefits, and §140503 for a list of excluded benefits.

44. It is unclear whether providers would be permitted to bargain as a unit, which would require a waiver from existing antitrust laws. The language of the bill is somewhat vague: "The state shall actively supervise and regulate a system of payments whereby groups of fee-for-service physicians are authorized to *select representatives of their specialties* to negotiate with [CHIS], pursuant to §140209. Nothing in this division shall be construed to allow collective action against [CHIS]" §140000.1(b) 16–21 (emphasis added).

45. As outlined in the powers of the commissioner (§140102), the language broadly states that the commissioner will "negotiate for or set rates, fees and prices involving any aspect of the [CHIS] and establish procedures thereto" [§140102 (y) 7–9]. In the same section, the language regarding pharmaceuticals reads differently, stating that the commissioner will "utilize the purchasing power of the state to negotiate price discounts for prescription drugs and durable and nondurable medical equipment for use by the [CHIS] system" (§140102 [dd] 22–25).

46. §140000.6.

47. Sheils and Haught (2005).

48. California State Senate (2005); Sheils and Haught (2005).

49. Anderson et al. (2003); Anderson et al. (2005).

50. Patel and Rushefsky (2002); Tuohy (1999; 2002).

51. Abelson et al. (2004); Blendon et al. (2003); Deber (2003); Light (2003); Tuohy (1999; 2002).

52. Kotlikoff and Hagist (2005).

53. For example, see Canada NewsWire (2005).

54. "The Commissioner shall . . . implement eligibility standards for the system, including guidelines to prevent an influx of persons to the state for the purpose of obtaining medical care" (California Health Insurance Reliability Act, §140102 [gg] 32).

55. Sheils and Haught (2005).

56. Schneider (2003).

57. California Health Insurance Reliability Act, §140102 (r)–(t).

58. Sloan (1988); Lanning, Morrisey, and Ohsfeldt (1991); Antel, Ohsfeldt, and Becker (1995); Conover and Sloan (1998).)

59. Blendon et al. (2003).

60. Abelson et al. (2004).

61. Ibid., 191.

62. Carroll et al. (2005).

63. Judis (2006).

64. Coase (1988); Hart (1995); Furubotn and Richter (1997); Williamson (1991; 1999).

65. See, for example, Schwartz and Watson (2003).

66. Williamson (1991).

67. According to Williamson (1991), coordinated adaptation refers to "the conscious, deliberate, and purposeful efforts to craft adaptive internal coordinating mechanisms" (103).

68. Nelson and Winter (1982); Milgrom and Roberts (1990; 1992); Williamson (1991); Akerlof and Kranton (2005).

69. Birla (2005).

70. Cutler and McClellan (2001); Lichtenberg (2001).

71. Lichtenberg (2001).

72. Heclo (1977, 395).
73. Moe (1991, 123).
74. See, for example, Wilson (1989); Moe (1990; 1991); and Williamson (1999).
75. Heclo (1977).
76. Collins-Nakai (2005, A17).
77. Robinson (2001, 1051).
78. Ibid.
79. Ibid.
80. Ibid.
81. See, for example, Whitney, McGuire, and McCullough (2004).
82. Robinson (2001).
83. See, for example, Alexander and Lantos (2006).
84. Johnson and Christensen (2004).

Chapter 3: Competition in Hospital Markets: The Case of Specialty Hospitals

1. The moratorium was enacted by Congress as part of the Medicare Prescription Drug, Improvement and Modernization Act of 2003 (MMA). It became effective when the law was signed on December 8, 2003, and was allowed to expire June 8, 2005, following extensive committee debate. However, new legislation allows CMS to suspend issuance of new provider numbers to specialty hospitals while the issue is further studied (Hyland 2005).

2. Casalino, Devers, and Brewster (2003); Shactman (2005); Guterman (2006); Kahn (2006); American Hospital Association (2006).

3. We conducted a survey of the seventy specialty hospitals belonging to the American Surgical Hospital Association. The survey achieved a 50 percent response rate, but the incorporation of existing data from ASHA resulted in item-level response rates ranging from 50 to 90 percent. Descriptive statistics from the survey are provided in table 3-2.

4. Throughout the chapter, we describe findings from case studies of five surgical hospitals, two in central California and three in South Dakota. These states were chosen due to the relatively high proportion and maturity of specialty hospitals. Site visits generally involved question-and-answer sessions with all levels of the management team (including physician-owners) at each facility, followed by tours. Also provided were documents on management strategy, quality assurance, consumer satisfaction, physician ownership, and cost management. The main goal of the site visits was to improve our understanding of the layout and functioning of specialty hospitals.

5. Skinner (1974); Womack, Jones, and Roos (1990); Essletzbichler (2003); Gollop and Monahan (1991).

6. Myers (1998); Eastaugh (2001); Robinson (2005).

7. For example, the General Accounting Office defines specialty hospitals as those that "tend to focus on patients with specific medical conditions or who need surgical procedures" (U.S. General Accounting Office 2003b).

8. Refer to chapter 2, "Impact of Competition" (39).

9. U.S. Congress. Senate. Committee on Homeland Security and Governmental Affairs. Subcommittee on Federal Financial Management (2005).

10. Ibid.

11. U.S. General Accounting Office (2003a).

12. U.S. General Accounting Office (2003a; 2003b); U.S. Congress. Senate. Committee on Homeland Security and Governmental Affairs. Subcommittee on Federal Financial Management (2005); U.S. Department of Health and Human Services. Centers for Medicare and Medicaid Services (2005).

13. U.S. General Accounting Office (2003a).

14. Baum (1999); Romano and Kirchheimer (2001); Eastaugh (2001); Smith (2002); Urquhart and O'Dell (2004); Herzlinger (2004a; 2004c); Lo Sasso et al. (2004).

15. Dranove (1987).

16. Robinson (2005, 58).

17. Walker (1998); Casalino, Pham, and Bazzoli (2004); Casey (2004); Rohack (2004); Iglehart (2005).

18. Casalino, Pham, and Bazzoli (2004, 86).

19. Cowing, Holtmann, and Powers (1983); Vita (1990); Gaynor and Anderson (1995); Keeler and Ying (1996); Dranove (1998b); Li and Rosenman (2001a; 2001b).

20. Cram, Rosenthal, and Vaughan-Sarrazin (2005).

21 Panzar and Willig (1981).

22. Menke (1997).

23. Fournier and Mitchell (1992).

24. Sinay and Campbell (1995).

25. Rozek (1988); Li and Rosenman (2001a).

26. Skinner (1974, 115).

27. March (1996); Nooteboom (2000); Greve (2003).

28. Nelson and Winter (1982).

29. Chandler (1992); Wruck and Jensen (1994); Greve (2003).

30. Teece et al. (1994); Teece and Pisano (1994); Hill (1994); Danneels (2002). For example, focusing on core competencies has been associated with improved supply-chain management (primarily through standardization), simplified human resource management, and streamlined production scheduling.

31. Milgrom and Roberts (1990).

32. Teece et al. (1994, 17).

33. Almeida, Dokko, and Rosenkopf (2003).

34. According to the survey results, 92 percent of specialty hospitals reported conducting systematic customer satisfaction surveys.

35. The relationship between core competencies and hospital efficiency is relatively under-studied. General discussions are provided by Eastaugh (2001; 1992); Snail and Robinson (1998); Douglas and Ryman (2003); Coddington, Palmquist, and Trollinger (1985); Porter and Teisberg (2004); Herzlinger (2004b); Moore (1990); and Walker and Rosko (1988).

36. Shortell, Morrison, and Hughes (1989).

37. Eastaugh (2001).

38. Douglas and Ryman (2003).

39. Walker (1998); Baum (1999); Daus (2000); Casey (2004); Wolski (2004); Zuckerman (2004). MedCath's description of their facilities is apposite: "Externally, MedCath's heart hospitals appear typical; however, a step inside reveals important differences: Physicians empowered to make decisions about hospital operations; state-of-the-art operating rooms; cutting-edge equipment and technology; centrally located services such as radiology, pharmacy and laboratories; nursing stations strategically positioned to allow better patient monitoring; and large, single-patient, fully equipped rooms that avoid unnecessary patient moves and permit family members to remain overnight. Above all, physicians and nurses freed from bureaucratic and administrative chores so they can devote a majority of their time and energy directly to caring for their patients" (MedCath Corporation 2006).

40. At least one report on specialty hospitals, based on interviews with providers and health plans, speculated that production efficiencies may be offset by "medical arms race" overproduction through the replication of existing community services (Berenson, Bazzoli, and Au 2006). There is no empirical evidence to support such a conjecture.

41. Kovner et al. (2002) found that the median number of RN hours per adjusted patient day was 6.43 for the study's 534 general hospitals. For the five specialty hospitals we visited, RN hours per adjusted patient day ranged from 10 to 15 hours per patient day. Ideally, however, the appropriate comparison would be between cardiac and orthopedic units of specialty hospitals and cardiac and orthopedic units of general hospitals. We know of no such studies, and we were not able to identify a source of data on nurse staffing ratios within specific units of general hospitals.

42. U.S. General Accounting Office (2003a; 2003b); Cram, Rosenthal, and Vaughan-Sarrazin (2005); Barro, Huckman, and Kessler (2005); Greenwald et al. (2006). In a study conducted by Lewin Group for the MedCath Corporation, Dobson (2004) found case-mix results counter to the GAO study and Cram et al. (2004). The Lewin Group found that MedCath cardiac hospitals have a 21 percent higher case-mix severity for cardiac patients compared to their community general hospital peers. The differences in findings are likely attributable to differences in the sample and the measurement of severity or complexity. For example, the Dobson study used DRG weights to measure severity, whereas Cram et al. used a predicted mortality model based on age and presence of seven comorbid conditions. However, the Dobson findings are consistent with anecdotal and empirical evidence that admitting physicians may

perceive specialized facilities as being more appropriate for complicated cases, due in part to the positive volume–outcome relationship (Baum 1999; Magid et al. 2000).

43. Winter (2003).

44. Hillner, Smith, and Desch (2000); Halm, Lee, and Chassin (2002); Shahian and Normand (2003).

45. Cram, Rosenthal, and Vaughan-Sarrazin (2005).

46. Epstein et al. (2004). An additional limitation is that the causal relationship between volume and outcome is unclear: Do patients treated at high-volume hospitals achieve better outcomes because of learning and practice (the "practice makes perfect" hypothesis of Hughes et al. 1988), or do hospitals with better reputations attract higher volumes of patients (the "selective referral" hypothesis)? Some recent studies have used instrumental variable techniques to disentangle these effects; one such paper found strong evidence of the "practice makes perfect" hypothesis for coronary artery bypass graft surgery (Gaynor, Seider, and Vogt 2005). There is some evidence that both hypotheses explain differences in outcomes; nonetheless, taken together, they explain a relatively small proportion of the overall variation in patient outcomes (Luft 1980; Luft, Hunt, and Maerki 1987).

47. Dobson (2004).

48. Barro, Huckman, and Kessler (2005).

49. Cram, Rosenthal, and Vaughan-Sarrazin (2005).

50. See, for example, Warner, Shields, and Chute (1993) and Mezei and Chung (1999).

51. Greenwald et al. (2006, 106).

52. Spetz et al. (2000).

53. Kovner et al. (2002); Lang et al. (2004); U.S. Department of Health and Human Services. Agency for Healthcare Research and Quality (2004); Mark et al. (2004).

54. Chief Executive Officer of a large specialty hospital in California. Personal communication (November 19, 2004)

55. Walker (1998); Fine (2004); Iqbal and Taylor (2001).

56. See, for example, O'Donnell (1993); Baum (1999); Leung (2000); Urquhart and O'Dell (2004); Hoffer Gittell (2004); Herzlinger (2004b; 2004c).

57. This section relies on an unpublished analysis of the competitive effects of specialty hospitals by Schneider et al. (2005).

58. Medicare cost report data and information from CMS (2006a).

59. The Area Resource File is a national county-level health resources information system containing detailed information on health professions, health training programs, health facilities, measures of resource scarcity, health status, economic activity, and socioeconomic and environmental characteristics. The dataset contains information on more than six thousand variables for each U.S. county. More information about the Area Resource File is available at http://www.arfsys.com (accessed June 5, 2006).

60. Profit rates were calculated as the difference between gross patient care revenue and total patient care costs (that is, net income from patient care activities), divided by gross patient care revenue. Mean profit margins reported here are somewhat lower than those reported elsewhere, for two reasons: (1) For the purposes of this study, profit margins are based on patient care revenue rather than total revenue; and (2) profit margins are aggregated to the county or MSA level.

61. Kumbhakar (1996).

62. Younis and Forgione (2005).

63. U.S. Bureau of Labor Statistics (2004).

64. The HHI is calculated by summing the squares of each firm's market share in the county; that is, $HHI = \sum^i 100 \ast s_i^2$, where s denotes the market share of firm i. This method allows for firms with relatively large market share (for example, 60 percent) to be more heavily weighted in the index.

65. We base this assumption on several sources. Dranove and the FTC have emphasized that hospital market areas need to be reconsidered in an era of dense managed care penetration, the rationale being that restricted enrollee choice leads to longer patient travel distances (Dranove 1998a; U.S. Federal Trade Commission and U.S. Department of Justice 2004). However, these authors and others (see, for example, Mobley and Frech 1998) also argue that managed care must be responsive to desire for local access, and that selective contracting works best when providers are in competition for the same pool of patients. Thus, as the FTC has argued, hospital geographic markets are "local" in scope. Supporting this finding, Mobley and Frech (1998) found that average travel distances to U.S. general hospitals were about 7 miles. The average county size in the United States is approximately 1,200 square miles; thus, by choosing the county as the relevant geographic market, we are likely capturing the vast majority of the market.

66. Baltagi (1995); Hsiao (1986).

67. MedPAC (2003a; 2003b).

68. The results for the specialty-hospital indicator variables were also positive and significant in exploratory models where the data were aggregated to the county and MSA level (that is, the county or MSA served as the unit of observation). In those exogenous entry fixed-effects models, the presence of any specialty hospital in the market was consistently associated with 2–3 percent higher general-hospital operating margins.

69. U.S. Federal Trade Commission and U.S. Department of Justice (2003; 2004).

70. Acute-care hospitals' implicit obligation to serve the community is based on two policies: the Hospital Survey and Construction Act of 1946 and nonprofit tax exemption. The nominal intent of the Hospital Survey and Construction Act of 1946 (commonly known as the Hill-Burton Act) was to bolster the relatively underdeveloped postwar hospital industry by requiring states "to develop programs for the construction of such public and other nonprofit hospitals that will, in conjunction with

existing facilities, afford the necessary physical facilities for furnishing adequate hospital, clinic, and similar services to all their people" (42 U.S.C., § 291).

71. Fournier and Campbell (1997); Schneider (2003).

72. See generally Lewin and Altman (2000).

73. Kane and Wubbenhorst (2000). A summary of these issues can also be found in Nancy Kane's recent testimony to the Subcommittee on Oversight of the U.S. House Committee on Ways and Means (U.S. Congress. House of Representatives. Committee on Ways and Means 2004).

74. American Hospital Association (2005).

75. Greenwald et al. (2006, 116).

76. Morrisey (1994).

77. This is a common occurrence in most industries. In the language of the current debate, this would be considered cream-skimming. An important question is whether it is optimal policy to discourage triaging of care across settings according to intensity, given the extensive literature on the cost and quality benefits associated with moving patients from inpatient to outpatient settings following the implementation of Medicare's PPS.

78. Currently, fourteen states have no CON programs, and another six maintain CON programs only for long-term care (Michigan Department of Community Health 2003).

79. Sloan and Steinwald (1980).

80. Lanning, Morrisey, and Ohsfeldt (1991); Antel, Ohsfeldt, and Becker (1995).

81. The poor performance of CON is attributed to four factors: the administrative burden associated with determining appropriateness of new investments; the potential for CON laws to create and maintain hospital cartels by erecting barriers to new hospital entrants; the susceptibility of the CON process to industry influence (see, for example, Payton and Powsner 1980); and the potentially suboptimal input allocation induced by the CON constraint on the use of capital inputs.

82. Conover and Sloan (1998). Some studies (for example, Vaughan-Sarrazin et al. 2002) have found that CON programs can be used to enhance patient outcomes by concentrating services in high-volume facilities. These studies are limited, however, by the causality problem and the lack of analysis of whether improvement in outcomes compensates for the net social welfare losses associated with barriers to market entry (U.S. Federal Trade Commission and U.S. Department of Justice 2004).

83. U.S. Federal Trade Commission and U.S. Department of Justice (2004, 23).

84. Vladeck (2006).

85. Lewin and Altman (2000, 215–16).

86. Morrison and Winston (1986).

87. Winston (1998); Peltzman and Winston (2000). Interestingly, Altman, Shactman, and Eilat (2006, 11) use the airline example to make precisely the opposite point, choosing instead to focus on the perceived attenuation in airline service postderegulation. They argue that if U.S. hospitals are unable to continue cross-subsidizing

low-margin services, they "could begin to resemble U.S. airlines: severely cutting costs, eliminating services, and suffering financial instability." But the authors' nostalgia for the apex of airline regulation and the prominence of stable "legacy" airlines clouds the facts. Post-deregulation changes in the airline industry have resulted in declines in real prices and net operating costs on the order of 10–30 percent (Winston 1998). Reductions in real prices have led to increased access as significantly larger number of people can now afford to fly (Keeler 1991; Morrison and Winston 1986; 1995).

88. One of the criticisms of specialty hospitals is that many do not provide twenty-four-hour emergency services. But it is not clear whether any current means of funding emergency room services are optimal. From a societal perspective, it may be more economically efficient to fund and operate emergency rooms no differently than police and fire departments.

89. FitzHenry and Shultz (2000); Iezzoni (2003).

90. Mitchell and Sass (1995); Lynk and Longley (2002); Kouri, Parsons, and Alpert (2002); Zientek (2003); U.S. Congress. Congressional Research Service. Domestic Social Policy Division (2004).

91. Mitchell and Sass (1995).

92. The Stark Amendments (1989 for Phase 1 and 1993 for Phase 2) are federal laws prohibiting physicians from referring Medicare and Medicaid patients to facilities (excluding inpatient hospitals) if the physician or an immediate family member of the physician has a direct or indirect financial interest in the entity providing services.

93. Stout and Warner (2003); Rohack (2004); U.S. Congress. Congressional Research Service. Domestic Social Policy Division (2004).

94. Kouri, Parsons, and Alpert (2002); Zientek (2003).

95. Moore (2003).

96. Kouri, Parsons, and Alpert (2002); Zientek (2003).

97. U.S. General Accounting Office (2003a).

98. It should also be noted that high variation in utilization and referral patterns exist without respect to physician ownership. For example, Weinstein et al. (2004) recently observed significant variation in utilization patterns for major surgery for degenerative diseases of the hip, knee, and spine in several South Florida hospital referral regions where there are no physician-owned specialty hospitals.

99. Wilson (2006).

100. Snail and Robinson (1998); Cuellar and Gertler (2006).

101. Burns, Andersen, and Shortell (1990); Romano (2005).

Chapter 4: Competition in Health Insurance Markets: The Case of Managed Care Reform

1. Notes recorded during California Senate Insurance Committee hearing, January 17, 2001.

2. Weil (1996); Jorgensen and Weil (1998).

3. Rogal and Stenger (2001).

4. Gold, Hurley, and Lake (2001).

5. See, for example, Schneider (2003).

6. Breyer (1982).

7. Barnes (1947).

8. The term "economic regulation" is used to distinguish between regulations aimed exclusively at quality and safety and those aimed at controlling the economic aspects of markets and firms, including market structure, firm operations, and finances. The latter variety of regulation is also referred to as "public-utility regulation," owing to its initial application in traditional utility industries, such as electricity, water, and natural gas.

9. Joskow and Rose (1989).

10. Coase (1988); Williamson (1985; 1991).

11. Goldberg (1976); Priest (1993); Williamson (1996).

12 Bernstein (1955); Peltzman (1976); Owen (1985).

13. Becker (1983); Keeler (1984).

14. Heclo (1979); Wright (1996).

15. Peltzman and Winston (2000).

16. Baumol and Klevorick (1970); Breyer (1982); Winston et al. (1990); Keeler (1991); Winston (1993); Vietor (1994); Peltzman and Winston (2000).

17. See, for example, Butler (1993); Friedman and Coffey (1993); Antel, Ohsfeldt, and Becker (1995); Schneider (2003).

18. Winston (1998).

19. Morrison and Winston (1986); Winston et al. (1990); Newberry (1999).

20. Institute of Medicine (1974).

21. Noble and Brennan (1999); Zelman (1999); Blendon et al. (1999); Thorpe (1999).

22. Pauly and Nicholson (1999).

23. Stauffer (2000); Rogal and Stenger (2001).

24. Havighurst (1995); Korobkin (1999); Pauly and Berger (1999).

25. Sloan and Hall (2002).

26. Based on data from California Association of Health Plans (1997–2001) and legislation listed and described at the Legislative Council of California's website www.leginfo.ca.gov (queried most recently on January 15, 2006).

27. Roth and Kelch (2001).

28. Porter (2004); Keating (2004).

29. For example, the stated overall mission of PBGH is "to improve the quality and availability of health care while moderating costs," and the first stated subgoal is to "enable purchasers to make value based choices that promote efficient delivery and equitable access to high-quality care" (PBGH 2006).

30. The principal constituents of the California Healthcare Association are California's approximately five hundred hospitals.

31. Morrisey (2000).

32. Kenkel (1994).

33. Tengs et al. (1995); Kenkel (2000); Pignone et al. (2002).

34. Cooper and Green (1991); Schneider (1999); U.S. Congress. Congressional Budget Office (1999); Emmons and Wozniak (1999); Baker and McClellan (2001).

35. Miller and Luft (1997); Reschovsky and Kemper (2000); Miller and Luft (2002).

36. Baker and McClellan (2001).

37. See, for example, Douglas and Miller (1974).

38. Encinosa (2001).

39. Gruber (1994); Jensen and Morrisey (1999).

40. Pauly and Berger (1999); Lansky (2002).

41. Barents Group LLC (1997); Schneider (1999); Emmons and Wozniak (1999). Also see Dobson and Steinberg (1999) for a discussion of these findings.

42. Schneider (1999); Noether (2000).

43. Walshe and Shortell (2004, 93).

44. Joskow (1991; 1997).

45. Walshe and Shortell (2004).

46. See, for example, U.S. Federal Trade Commission and U.S. Department of Justice (2004); Conover and Sloan (1998); Havighurst (2005).

Chapter 5: Competition in Pharmaceutical Markets: The Case of Prescription Drug Marketing

1. Hollon (1999, 382).

2. Abramson (2005, 154).

3. Ibid., 151–52.

4. Nelson (1974); Schmalensee (1978).

5. Nelson (1974).

6. See, for example, Stivers and Tremblay (2005).

7. Calfee (2002).

8. 1996 and 1997 data from IMS Health (2003); 2004 data from IMS Health (2006b).

9. Pines (1999); Palumbo and Mullins (2002).

10. Pines (1999).

11. Kaphingst et al. (2004); Huh and Cude (2004).

12. Pines (1999).

13. See, for example, Clarke (2004).

14. Robinson et al. (2004).

15. Calfee (2002).

16. Lyles (2002).

17. Calfee (2002).

18. Of course, consumers do receive detailed information about risks through the patient package insert (PPI)—a several-page-long, text-intensive document, often folded into about a 2" x 2" square and included with the prescription. However, this document is obtained *after* a prescription has been filled, and therefore cannot inform the consumer about risks before the drug is prescribed.

19. Standardized patients are commonly used in clinical training. These are individuals without a specific health condition who present to physicians with an identical array of clinical information (such as medical history) on their charts and are trained to use the same specific words when describing their symptoms.

20. Kravitz et al. (2005).

21. See, for example, Ohsfeldt, Lage, and Rajagopalan (2005).

22. Kravitz et al. (2005, 1998, table 1).

23. See, for example, Donohue et al. (2004).

24. Zachry, Dalen, and Jackson (2003).

25. Robinson et al. (2004). It should be noted that current FDA regulations relating to the extent of scientific support for cost information or "claims" effectively preclude the use of any cost information in DTCA for almost all prescription drugs (Palumbo and Mullins 2002). Similar requirements also substantially limit the extent of information for alternative treatments permitted in DTCA.

26. U.S. Food and Drug Administration. Center for Drug Evaluation and Research (2003).

27. Palumbo and Mullins (2002).

28. National Institute for Health Care Management Foundation (2001).

29. Data for U.S. sales were computed by the authors from information provided in company annual reports.

30. Manning and Keith (2001).

31. National Institute for Health Care Management Foundation (2001).

32. Health expenditure data for 2000 are from the CMS (2006b).

33. Calfee (2002).

34. Hensley (2005).

35. Findlay (2002); Rosenthal et al. (2002); Vogel, Ramachandran, and Zachry (2003).

36. Millstein (2003).

37. Calfee (2002); Lichtenberg (2003).

38. Wolfe (2002).

39. Abramson (2005) devotes an entire chapter in his book to this topic.

40. Bextra did not enter the U.S. market until 2001 (U.S. Congress. House of Representatives. Committee on Government Reform 2005).

41. National Institute for Health Care Management Foundation (2001).

42. 2000 data from National Institute for Health Care Management Foundation (2001), 2003 data from IMS Health (2004). Sales of Celebrex fell to $2.2 billion

in 2005 (IMS Health, 2006a). Vioxx was withdrawn from the market in 2004.

43. Retail prices per Drugstore.com, inc. (2006).

44. Whittle (2000).

45. Tramer et al. (2000).

46. Wolfe et al. (1999, 1889).

47. U.S. Congress. House of Representatives. Committee on Government Reform (2005).

48. See, for example, Dalen (2002).

49. This is an example of the classic issue of limited "external validity" for clinical trials—the treatment "efficacy" observed in clinical trials may not translate into treatment "effectiveness" in usual clinical practice (because the patients being treated in practice may differ from those included in clinical trials or receive treatments that differ from the protocol-specified treatment in clinical trials).

50. Harley and Wagner (2003).

51. Bombardier, Laine, and Reicin (2000).

52. U.S. Congress. House of Representatives. Committee on Government Reform (2005).

53. Bresalier (2005).

54. U.S. Congress. House of Representatives. Committee on Government Reform (2005).

55. U.S. Food and Drug Administration. Center for Drug Evaluation and Research (2005).

56. U.S. Congress. House of Representatives. Committee on Government Reform (2005).

57. Mitchell and Warner (2006), Kearney et al. (2006).

58. Hill (1958, 300).

59. Oberholzer-Gee and Inarndar (2004).

60. Calfee (2005); Curfman, Morrissey, and Drazen (2005); Frank (2005); *New York Times* (2005); *Wall Street Journal* (2006).

61. Ironically, the FDA did not permit information about a lower risk of gastrointestinal adverse effects to be included in DTCA until 2003 (U.S. Congress. House of Representatives. Committee on Government Reform 2005).

62. Ibid.

63. Doshi et al. (2004).

64. Palumbo and Mullins (2002).

65. *Central Hudson Gas & Elec. Corp. v. Public Service Commission of New York*, 447 U.S. 557 (1980).

66. See *Lorillard Tobacco Co. v. Reilly*, 533 U.S. 525 (2001), and *Coyne Beahm Inc. v. FDA*, 966 F. Supp. 1374 (M.D.N.C. 1997). However, the latter case was related to the FDA's lack of regulatory authority rather than the issue of commercial speech.

67. See *Thompson v. Western States Medical Center*, 535 U.S. 357 (2002) for *Central Hudson* criteria applied to a form of prescription drug promotion.

68. Wolfe (2002).

69. Promotion in the form of distributing pens, coffee mugs, and other items emblazoned with a drug logo to physicians also is prohibited, because such items do not include full risk information.

70. Calfee (2003).

71. Dubois (2003).

72. Donohue et al. (2004).

73. Calfee (2002).

74. Dranove (2000).

Conclusions and Policy Implications

1. See, for example, Nelson (1974) and Schmalensee (1978).

2. Coase (1988); Hart (1995); Furubotn and Richter (1997); Williamson (1991; 1999).

3. Anderson and Tushman (1990); Utterbach (1994, chapter 2); Levinthal (1996); Nooteboom (2000, chapter 4).

4. Levinthal (1996, 197–98).

5. Pauly (2005, 1524).

6. Havighurst (1995; 2000).

7. Havighurst (1995, 4).

8. Williamson (1991); Easterbrook and Fischel (1993); Speidel (1993).

9. Dowd (2005); Hall and Havighurst (2005).

10. See, for example, Chao (2005).

11. Nyman (2004).

References

Aaron, H. J. 2003. The Costs of Health Care Administration in the United States and Canada—Questionable Answers to a Questionable Question. *New England Journal of Medicine* 349 (8): 801, 803.

Abelson, J., M. Mendelsohn, J. N. Lavis, S. G. Morgan, P. Forest, and M. Swinton. 2004. Canadians Confront Health Care Reform. *Health Affairs* 23 (3): 186–93.

Abramson, J. 2005. *Overdosed America: The Broken Promise of American Medicine: How the Pharmaceutical Companies are Corrupting Science, Misleading Doctors, and Threatening Your Health.* New York: Harper.

Akerlof, G. A., and R. E. Kranton. 2005. Identity and the Economics of Organizations. *Journal of Economic Perspectives* 19 (1): 9–32.

Alexander, G. C., and J. D. Lantos. 2006. The Doctor-Patient Relationship in the Post-Managed Care Era. *American Journal of Bioethics* 6 (1): 29–32.

Almeida, P., G. Dokko, and L. Rosenkopf. 2003. Startup Size and the Mechanisms of External Learning: Increasing Opportunity and Decreasing Ability? *Research Policy* 32 (2):301–16.

Alter, D. A., A. Basinkski, E. Cohen, and C. D. Naylor. 1999. Fairness in the Coronary Angiography Queue. *CMAJ* 161 (7): 813–17.

Altman, S. H., D. Shactman, and E. Eilat. 2006. Could U.S. Hospitals Go the Way of U.S. Airlines? *Health Affairs* 25 (1): 11–21.

American Enterprise Institute. 2005. Counting the Uninsured: Three Surveys, Three Answers. Presentations at AEI panel discussion. Washington, D.C., September 9. Available at http://www.aei.org/events/eventID.1145,filter.all/event_detail.asp (accessed May 24, 2006).

American Hospital Association. 1997. *Hospital Statistics.* Chicago, Ill.: Health Forum LLC.

———. 2004. *Hospital Statistics.* Chicago, Ill.: Health Forum LLC.

———. 2005. Uncompensated Care Costs Grow to $25 Billion. *Healthcare Financial Management* 59 (1): 21.

———. 2006. *The AHA's 2006 Advocacy Agenda.* Chicago, Ill.: American Hospital Association.

Anders, G. 2001. A National Overview. In *The Challenge of Regulating Managed Care*, ed. J. E. Billi and G. B. Agrawal. Ann Arbor, Mich.: The University of Michigan Press.

Anderson, G. F., P. S. Hussey, B. K. Frogner, and H. R. Waters. 2005. Health Spending in the United States and the Rest of the Industrialized World. *Health Affairs* 24 (4): 903–14.

Anderson, G. F., U. Reinhardt, P. Hussy, and V. Petrosyan. 2003. It's the Prices, Stupid: Why the United States is So Different from Other Countries. *Health Affairs* 22 (3): 89–105.

Anderson, P., and M. L. Tushman. 1990. Technological Discontinuities and Dominant Designs: A Cyclical Model of Technological Change. *Administrative Science Quarterly* 35 (1): 604–33.

Antel, J. J., R. L. Ohsfeldt, and E. R. Becker. 1995. State Regulation and Hospital Cost Performance. *Review of Economics and Statistics* 77 (3): 416–22.

Aoki, M. 1990. Toward an Economic Model of the Japanese Firm. *Journal of Economic Literature* 28 (March): 1–27.

Appleby, J. 2004. Scales Tipping Against Tax-Exempt Hospitals. *USA Today*, August 24, 2004.

Arnesen, K. E., J. Erikssen, and K. Stavem. 2002. Gender and Socioeconomic Status as Determinants of Waiting Time for Inpatient Surgery in a System with Implicit Queue Management. *Health Policy* 62 (3): 329–41.

Arrow, K. J. 1963. Uncertainty and the Welfare Economics of Medical Care. *American Economic Review* 53 (5): 941–73.

Asch, S. M., E. A. Kerr, J. Keesey, J. L. Adams, C. M. Setodji, S. Malik, and E. A. McGlynn. 2006. Who Is at Greatest Risk for Receiving Poor-Quality Care? *New England Journal of Medicine* 354 (11): 1147–56.

Baker, L. C., and M. B. McClellan. 2001. Managed Care, Health Care Quality, and Regulation. *Journal of Legal Studies* 30 (2): 715–41.

Baltagi, B. H. 1995. *Economic Analysis of Panel Data.* New York: Wiley.

Barents Group, LLC. 1997. The Effects of Legislation Affecting Managed Care on Health Plan Costs. Prepared for the American Association of Health Plans, Washington, D.C.

Barnard, C. I. 1964. *The Functions of the Executive.* Cambridge, Mass.: Harvard University Press.

Barnes, I. R. 1947. *The Economics of Public Utility Regulation.* New York: F. S. Crofts.

Barro, J. R., R. S. Huckman, and D. P. Kessler. 2005. The Effects of Cardiac Specialty Hospitals on the Cost and Quality of Medical Care. NBER Working Paper No. 11707. Cambridge, Mass.: National Bureau of Economic Research.

Bartlett, D. L., and J. B. Steele. 2004. *Critical Condition: How Health Care in America Became Big Business—and Bad Medicine.* New York: Doubleday.

Baum, N. H. 1999. "Focused Factories" Could Be Wave of the Future. *Urology Times* 27 (3): 22.

Baumol, W., and A. Klevorick. 1970. Input Choices and Rate-of-Return Regulation: An Overview of the Discussion. *Bell Journal of Economics and Management Science* 1 (2): 162–90.

Becker, G. 1983. A Theory of Competition Among Pressure Groups for Political Influence. *Quarterly Journal of Economics* 98 (3): 371–400.

Bell, C. M., M. Crystal, A. S. Detsky, and D. A. Redelmeier. 1999. Shopping Around for Hospital Services: A Comparison of the United States and Canada. *Journal of the American Medical Association* 279 (13): 1015–17.

Berenson, R. A., G. J. Bazzoli, and M. Au. 2006. Do Specialty Hospitals Promote Price Competition? In *Issue Brief No. 103*. Washington, D.C.: Center for Studying Health System Change.

Berger, M. C., D. A. Black, F. A. Scott, and A. Chandra. 1999. Health Insurance Coverage of the Unemployed: COBRA and the Potential Effects of Kassenbaum-Kennedy. *Journal of Policy Analysis and Management* 18 (3): 430–48.

Berndt, E. R. 2000. International Comparisons of Pharmaceutical Prices: What Do We Know, and What Does It Mean? *Journal of Health Economics* 19 (2): 283–87.

Bernstein, M. H. 1955. *Regulating Business by Independent Commission*. Princeton: Princeton University Press.

———. 1972. Independent Regulatory Agencies: A Perspective on Their Reform. *Annals of the American Academy of Political and Social Science* 400 (March): 14–26.

Birla, M. 2005. *FedEx Delivers: How the World's Leading Shipping Company Keeps Innovating and Outperforming the Competition*. Hoboken, N.J.: John Wiley and Sons.

Bishai, D. D., and H. C. Lang. 2000. The Willingness to Pay for Wait Reduction: The Disutility of Queues for Cataract Surgery in Canada, Denmark, and Spain. *Journal of Health Economics* 19 (2): 219–30.

Blendon, R. J., M. Brodie, J. M. Benson, D. E. Altman, L. Levitt, T. Hoff, and L. Hugick. 1999. The Public: Understanding the Managed Care Backlash. In *Regulating Managed Care: Theory, Practice, and Future Options*, ed. S. H. Altman, U. W. Reinhardt, and D. Shactman. San Francisco: Jossey-Bass.

Blendon, R. J., C. Schoen, C. M. DesRoches, R. Osborn, K. M. Scoles, and K. Zapert. 2002. Inequities in Health Care: A Five-Country Survey. *Health Affairs* 21 (3): 182–91.

Blendon, R. J., C. Schoen, C. M. DesRoches, R. Osborn, and K. Zapert. 2003. Common Concerns Amid Diverse Systems: Health Care Experiences in Five Countries. *Health Affairs* 22 (3): 106–21.

Boardman, A. E., and A. R. Vining. 1989. Ownership and Performance in Competitive Environments: A Comparison of the Performance of Private, Mixed and State-Owned Enterprises. *Journal of Law and Economics* 32 (1): 1–33.

Bodenheimer, T. 2003. The Movement for Universal Health Insurance: Finding Common Ground. *American Journal of Public Health* 93 (1): 112–15.

Bombardier, C., L. Laine, and A. Reicin. 2000. Comparison of Upper Gastrointestinal Toxicity or Rofecoxib and Naproxen in Patients with Rheumatoid Arthritis. *New England Journal of Medicine* 343 (21): 1520–28.

Bresalier, R. S. 2005. Cardiovascular Events Associated with Rofecoxib in a Colorectal Adenoma Chemoprevention Trial. *New England Journal of Medicine* 352 (11):1092–1102.

Breyer, S. 1982. *Regulation and Its Reform*. Cambridge, Mass.: Harvard University Press.

Brooks, J. M., C. P. Irwin, L. G. Hunsicker, M. J. Flanigan, E. A. Chrischilles, J. F. Pendergast. 2006. Effect of Dialysis Center Profit-Status on Patient Survival: A Comparison of Risk-Adjustment and Instrumental Variable Approaches. *Health Services Research* (forthcoming).

Burns, L. R., R. M. Andersen, and S. M. Shortell. 1990. The Effect of Hospital Control Strategies on Physician Satisfaction and Physician-Hospital Conflict. *Health Services Research* 25 (3): 527–60.

Butler, P. A. 1999. The Current Status of State and Federal Regulation. In *Regulating Managed Care: Theory, Practice, and Future Options*, ed. S. H. Altman, U. E. Reinhardt, and D. Shactman. San Francisco: Jossey-Bass.

Butler, S. M. 1993. The Fatal Attraction of Price Controls. In *Health Policy Reform: Competition and Controls*, ed. R. B. Helms. Washington, D.C.: AEI Press.

Calfee, J. E. 2002. Public Policy Issues in Direct-to-Consumer Advertising of Prescription Drugs. *Journal of Public Policy and Marketing* 21 (2):174–93.

———. 2003. What Do We Know About Direct-to-Consumer Advertising of Prescription Drugs? *Health Affairs* Web Exclusive (February 26): W3-116–19, http://www.healthaffairs.org (accessed May 24, 2006).

———. 2005. *The Vioxx Fallout*. Health Policy Outlook. AEI Online, September 30, http://www.aei.org/publications/pubID.23275/pub_detail.asp (accessed May 1, 2006).

California Association of Health Plans. 1997. *Profile and Annual Report*. Sacramento, Calif.

———. 1998. *Profile and Annual Report*. Sacramento, Calif.

———. 1999. *Profile and Annual Report*. Sacramento, Calif.

———. 2000. *Profile and Annual Report*. Sacramento, Calif.

———. 2001. *Profile and Annual Report*. Sacramento, Calif.

California State Senate. 2005. *Fact Sheet: SB 840 The California Health Insurance Reliability Act*. By S. J. Kuehl. Sacramento, Calif.: State of California.

Canada NewsWire. 2005. Health Care Spending to Reach $142 Billion This Year, December 7.

Cannon, M. F., and M. D. Tanner. 2005. *Healthy Competition: What's Holding Back Health Care and How to Free It*. Washington, D.C.: The Cato Institute.

Carroll, S. J., C. Krop, J. Arkes, P. A. Morrison, and A. Flanagan. 2005. *California's K–12 Public Schools*. Santa Monica, Calif.: RAND Corporation.

Casalino, L. P., K. J. Devers, and L. R. Brewster. 2003. Focused Factories? Physician-Owned Specialty Facilities. *Health Affairs* 22 (6): 56–57.

Casalino, L. P., H. Pham, and G. Bazzoli. 2004. Growth of Single-Specialty Medical Groups. *Health Affairs* 23 (2): 82–90.

Casey, J. 2004. The Case for Specialty Hospitals. *Modern Healthcare* 34 (47): 21–22.

Centers for Medicare and Medicaid Services. 1995. Medicare Hospital Status Reports. Washington, D.C.: Department of Health and Human Services.

———. 2002. Medicare Hospital Status Reports. Washington, D.C.: Department of Health and Human Services.

———. 2006a. Healthcare Cost Report Information System (HCRIS) 1997–2003. Washington, D.C.: Department of Health and Human Services. Available at http://www.cms.hhs.gov/CostReports/02_HospitalCostReport.asp. (accessed June 20, 2006).

———. 2006b. NHE Web Tables (Table 2), Office of the Actuary, National Health Statistics Group. http://www.cms.hhs.gov/NationalHealthExpendData/downloads/tables.pdf (accessed June 20, 2006).

Chandler, A. D. 1992. Organizational Capabilities and the Economic History of the Industrial Enterprise. *Journal of Economic Perspectives* 6 (3): 79–100.

Chao, L. 2005. Shopping for the Best Medical Prices. *Wall Street Journal*, September 8, 2005, D3.

Chernew, M., G. Gowrisankaran, and A. M. Fendrick. 2002. Payer Type and the Returns to Bypass Surgery: Evidence from Hospital Entry Behavior. *Journal of Health Economics* 21 (3): 451–74.

Clarke, P. M. 2004. A Model to Estimate the Lifetime Health Outcomes of Patients with Type 2 Diabetes: The United Kingdom Prospective Diabetes Study Outcomes Model. *Diabetologia* 47 (10): 1747–59.

Coase, R. H. 1988. *The Firm, the Market and the Law*. Chicago, Ill.: University of Chicago Press.

Coddington, D. C., L. E. Palmquist, and W. V. Trollinger. 1985. Strategies for Survival in the Hospital Industry. *Harvard Business Review* 63 (May–June): 129–38.

Collins-Nakai, R. 2005. Politics is Hurting Patients. *Ottawa Citizen*, November 14, 2005, A17.

Conover, C. J., and F. A. Sloan. 1998. Does Removing Certificate-of-Need Regulations Lead to a Surge in Health Care Spending? *Journal of Health Politics, Policy, and Law* 23 (3): 455–81.

Cooper, P. P., and K. Green. 1991. The Impact of State Laws on Managed Care. *Health Affairs* 10 (4): 161–69.

Copeland, C. 1998. Characteristics of the Nonelderly with Selected Sources of Health Insurance and Lengths of Uninsured Spells. EBRI Issue Brief No. 198. Washington D.C.: Employee Benefit Research Institute.

Cowing, T. G., A. G. Holtmann, and S. Powers. 1983. Hospital Cost Analysis: A Survey and Evaluation of Recent Studies. *Advances in Health Economics and Health Services Research* 4:257–303.

Cram, P. C., G. E. Rosenthal, and M. S. Vaughan-Sarrazin. 2004. Care of Patients Undergoing Angioplasty in Specialty and Non-Specialty Heart Hospitals: Cherry

Picking and/or Improved Outcomes? Paper presented at the 27th annual meeting of the Society of General Internal Medicine, May 12–14, Chicago, Ill.

———. 2005. Cardiac Revascularization in Specialty and General Hospitals. *New England Journal of Medicine* 352 (14): 1454–62.

Cuellar, A. E., and P. J. Gertler. 2006. Strategic Integration of Hospitals and Physicians. *Journal of Health Economics* 25 (1): 1–28.

Curfman, G. D., S. Morrissey, and J. M. Drazen. 2005. Expression of Concern: Bombardier et al., "Comparison of Upper Gastrointestinal Toxicity or Rofecoxib and Naproxen in Patients with Rheumatoid Arthritis." *New England Journal of Medicine* 353 (26): 2813–14.

Cutler, D. M. 2004. *Your Money or Your Life: Strong Medicine for America's Health Care System*. New York: Oxford University Press.

Cutler, D. M., and M. McClellan. 2001. Is Technological Change in Medicine Worth It? *Health Affairs* 20 (5): 11–29.

Dalen, J. E. 2002. Selective COX-2 Inhibitors, NSAIDs, Aspirin and Myocardial Infarction. *Archives of Internal Medicine* 162 (10): 1091–92.

Danneels, E. 2002. The Dynamics of Product Innovation and Firm Competencies. *Strategic Management Journal* 23 (12): 1095–1121.

Danzon, P. M. 1992. Hidden Overhead Costs: Is Canada's System Really Less Expensive? *Health Affairs* 11 (Spring): 21–43.

———. 1999. *Price Comparisons of Pharmaceuticals: A Review of U.S. and Cross-National Studies*. Washington, D.C.: AEI Press.

———. 2000. Liability for Medical Malpractice. In *Handbook of Health Economics*, vol. 1B, ed. A. J. Culyer and J. P. Newhouse. New York: Elsevier.

Danzon, P. M., and L. Chao. 2000. Cross-National Price Differences for Pharmaceuticals: How Large, and Why? *Journal of Health Economics* 19 (2): 159–95.

Daus, C. 2000. The Dream Team. *Orthopedic Technology Review* 2 (5), http://www.orthopedictechreview.com/issues/may00/pg24.htm (accessed May 24, 2006).

Davidoff, A. J., B. Garrett, and A. Yemane. 2001. *Medicaid-Eligible Adults Who Are Not Enrolled: Who Are They and Do They Get the Care They Need?* Washington, D.C.: The Urban Institute.

De Alessi, L. 1983. Property Rights, Transactions Costs, and X-Efficiency: An Essay in Economic Theory. *American Economic Review* 73 (1): 64–81.

Deber, R. B. 2003. Health Care Reform: Lessons From Canada. *American Journal of Public Health* 93 (1): 20–24.

Demsetz, H. 1967. Toward a Theory of Property Rights. *American Economic Review* 57 (2): 347–59.

Devereaux, P. J., P. T. L. Choi, C. Lacchetti, B. Weaver, H. J. Schunemann, and T. Haines. 2002. A Systematic Review and Meta-Analysis of Studies Comparing Mortality Rates of Private For-Profit and Private Not-For-Profit Hospitals. *Canadian Medical Association Journal* 166 (11): 1399–1406.

Devereaux, P. J., H. J. Schunemann, N. Ravindran, M. Bhandari, A. X. Garg, and P. T. L. Choi. 2002. Comparison of Mortality Between Private For-Profit and Private Not-For-Profit Hemodialysis Centers: A Systematic Review and Meta-Analysis. *Journal of the American Medical Association* 288 (19): 2249–57.

Dobson, A. 2004. *A Comparative Study of Patient Severity, Quality of Care and Community Impact at MedCath Heart Hospitals.* Washington, D.C.: Lewin Group.

Dobson, A., and C. Steinberg. 1999. The Cost of Regulation: How the Estimates Vary. In *Regulating Managed Care: Theory, Practice, and Future Options*, ed. S. H. Altman, U. E. Reinhardt, and D. Shactman. San Francisco: Jossey-Bass.

Docteur, E., H. Suppanz, and J. Woo. 2003. The US Health System: An Assessment and Prospective Directions for Reform. In Working Paper No. 350, OECD Economics Department. Paris, France: Organisation for Economic Co-operation and Development.

Donohue, J. M., E. R. Berndt, M. Rosenthal, A. M. Epstein, and R. G. Frank. 2004. Effects of Pharmaceutical Promotion on Adherence to the Treatment Guidelines for Depression. *Medical Care* 42 (12): 1176–85.

Doshi, J. A., N. Brandt, and B. Stuart. 2004. The Impact of Drug Coverage on COX-2 Inhibitor Use in Medicare. *Health Affairs* Web Exclusive (February 18): W4-94–105, http://www.healthaffairs.org (accessed May 24, 2006).

Douglas, G., and J. Miller. 1974. Quality Competition, Industry Equilibrium, and Efficiency in the Price Constrained Airline Market. *American Economic Review* 64 (4): 657–69.

Douglas, T. J., and J. A. Ryman. 2003. Understanding Competitive Advantage in the General Hospital Industry: Evaluating Strategic Competencies. *Strategic Management Journal* 24 (4): 333–47.

Dowd, B. E. 2005. Coordinated Agency Versus Autonomous Consumers in Health Services Markets. *Health Affairs* 24 (6): 1501–11.

Dranove, D. 1987. Rate-Setting by Diagnosis Related Groups and Hospital Specialization. *RAND Journal of Economics* 18 (3): 417–27.

———. 1998a. Market Definitions in Antitrust Analysis and Applications to Health Care. In *Managed Care and Changing Health Care Markets*, ed. M. A. Morrisey. Washington, D.C.: AEI Press.

———. 1998b. Economies of Scale in Non-Revenue Producing Cost Centers: Implications for Hospital Mergers. *Journal of Health Economics* 17 (1): 69–83.

———. 2000. *The Economic Evolution of American Health Care: From Marcus Welby to Managed Care.* Princeton, N.J.: Princeton University Press.

Dranove, D., M. Shanley, and C. Simon. 1992. Is Hospital Competition Wasteful? *RAND Journal of Economics* 23 (2): 247–62.

Drugstore.com, inc. 2006. available at http://www.drugstore.com/ (accessed June 26, 2006).

Duan, N. 1983. Smearing Estimate: A Nonparametric Retransformation Method. *Journal of the American Statistical Association* 78 (383): 605–10.

Dubois, R. W. 2003. Pharmaceutical Promotion: Don't Throw the Baby Out with the Bathwater. *Health Affairs* Web Exclusive (February 26): W3-96–103, http://www.healthaffairs.org (accessed May 24, 2006).

Eastaugh, S. R. 1992. Hospital Strategy and Financial Performance. *Health Care Management Review* 17 (3): 19–31.

———. 2001. Hospital Costs and Specialization: Benefits of Trimming Product Lines. *Journal of Health Care Finance* 28 (1): 61.

Easterbrook, F. H., and D. R. Fischel. 1993. Contract and Fiduciary Duty. *Journal of Law and Economics* 36 (1): 425–51.

Economic Research Initiative on the Uninsured. 2005. *Fast Facts: Characteristics of the Uninsured.* Ann Arbor: University of Michigan Press.

Emmons, D. W., and G. D. Wozniak. 1999. *Economic Impacts of Managed Care Reform.* Chicago, Ill.: Center for Health Policy Research/American Medical Association.

Encinosa, W. 2001. The Economics of Regulatory Mandates on the HMO Market. *Journal of Health Economics* 20 (1): 85–107.

Epstein, A. J., S. S. Rathore, K. G. M. Volpp, and H. M. Krumholz. 2004. Hospital Percutaneous Coronary Intervention Volume and Patient Mortality, 1998 to 2000: Does the Evidence Support the Current Procedure Volume Minimums? *Journal of the American College of Cardiology* 43 (10): 1755–62.

Essletzbichler, J. 2003. From Mass Production to Flexible Specialization: The Sectoral and Geographical Extent of Contract Work in U.S. Manufacturing. *Regional Studies* 37 (8): 753–71.

Findlay, S. 2002. Do Ads Really Drive Pharmaceutical Sales? The True Effects of DTC Advertising Remain a Mystery. *Marketing Health Services* 22 (1): 20–25.

Fine, A. 2004. The Specter of Specialty Hospitals, Part 1. *Hospitals & Health Networks*, June 22, http://www.hospitalconnect.com/hhnmag/jsp/articledisplay.jsp?dcrpath=AHA/PubsNewsArticle/data/040622HHN_Online_Fine&domain=HHNMAG (accessed April 18, 2006).

FitzHenry, F., and E. K. Shultz. 2000. Health-Risk-Assessment Tools Used to Predict Costs in Defined Populations. *Journal of Healthcare Information Management* 14 (2): 31–57.

Fournier, G. M., and E. S. Campbell. 1997. Indigent Care as Quid Pro Quo in Hospital Regulation. *Review of Economics and Statistics* 79 (4): 669–73.

Fournier, G. M., and J. M. Mitchell. 1992. Hospital Costs and Competition for Services. *Review of Economics and Statistics* 74 (4): 627–35.

Frank, T. 2005. *The Vioxx Litigation: Part I.* Working Paper No. 117, American Enterprise Institute, December 1, http://www.aei.org/research/liability/projectID.23/default.asp (accessed April 18, 2006).

Friedman, B., and R. Coffey. 1993. The Effectiveness of State Regulation of Hospital Revenue in the 1980s. In *Health Policy Reform: Competition and Controls*, ed. R. Helms. Washington, D.C.: AEI Press.

Fuchs, V. R., and J. S. Hahn. 1990. How Does Canada Do It? A Comparison of Expenditures for Physician Services in the United States and Canada. *New England Journal of Medicine* 323 (13): 844–90.

Fuhrmans, V. 2005. Health Insurers' New Target: Companies Go after the Uninsured with Cheaper Plans, Clever Marketing, But Benefits Are Sparse. *Wall Street Journal*, May 31, 2005, B1.

Furubotn, E. G., and S. Pejovich. 1972. Property Rights and Economic Theory: A Survey of Recent Literature. *Journal of Economic Literature* 10 (4): 1137–62.

Furubotn, E. G., and R. Richter. 1997. *Institutions and Economic Theory: The Contribution of the New Institutional Economics.* Ann Arbor, Mich.: University of Michigan Press.

Gaynor, M., and G. F. Anderson. 1995. Uncertain Demand, the Structure of Hospital Costs, and Cost of Empty Hospital Beds. *Journal of Health Economics* 14 (2): 291–317.

Gaynor, M., H. Seider, and W. B. Vogt. 2005. The Volume-Outcome Effect, Scale Economies, and Learning-by-Doing. *American Economic Review* 95 (2): 243–47.

Gold, M., R. Hurley, and T. Lake. 2001. Provider Organizations at Risk: A Profile of Major Risk-Bearing Intermediaries. *Health Affairs* 20 (2): 175–85.

Goldberg, V. P. 1976. Regulation and Administered Contracts. *Bell Journal of Economics and Management Science* 7 (2): 426–48.

Goldstein, R. B., M. J. Rotheram-Borus, M. O. Johnson, and L. S. Weinhardt. 2005. Insurance Coverage, Usual Source of Care, and Receipt of Clinically Indicated Care for Comorbid Conditions among Adults Living with Human Immunodeficiency Virus. *Medical Care* 43 (4): 401–10.

Gollop, F. M., and J. L. Monahan. 1991. A Generalized Index of Diversification: Trends in U.S. Manufacturing. *Review of Economics and Statistics* 73 (2): 318–30.

Grabowski, D. C., and R. A. Hirth. 2003. Competitive Spillovers Across Nonprofit and For-Profit Nursing Homes. *Journal of Health Economics* 22 (1): 1–22.

Grabowski, D. C., R. L. Ohsfeldt, and M. A. Morrisey. 2003. The Effects of CON Repeal on Medicaid Nursing Home and Long-Term Care Expenditures. *Inquiry* 40 (Summer): 146–57.

Greenwald, L., J. Cromwell, W. Adamache, S. Bernard, E. Drozd, E. Root, and K. J. Devers. 2006. Specialty Versus Community Hospitals: Referrals, Quality, and Community Benefits. *Health Affairs* 25 (1): 106–18.

Greenwald, R. 2005. *Wal-Mart: The High Cost of Low Price.* Brave New Films, Culver City, Calif., November 2005. Available at http://www.walmartmovie.com/ (accessed June 20, 2006)

Greve, H. R. 2003. *Organizational Learning from Performance Feedback: A Behavioral Perspective on Innovation and Change.* Cambridge: Cambridge University Press.

Gruber, J. 1994. The Incidence of Mandated Maternity Benefits. *American Economic Review* 84 (3): 622–41.

Guendelman, S., M. Wier, V. Angulao, and D. Oman. 2006. The Effects of Child-Only Insurance and Family Coverage on Health Care Access and Use: Recent

Findings Among Low Income Children in California. *Health Services Research* 41 (1): 125–47.

Guterman, S. 2006. Specialty Hospitals: A Problem or Symptom? *Health Affairs* 25 (1): 95–105.

Hadley, J., and J. D. Reschovsky. 2002. Small Firms' Demand for Health Insurance: The Decision to Offer Insurance. *Inquiry* 39 (2): 118.

Hall, M. A., and C. C. Havighurst. 2005. Reviving Managed Care With Health Savings Accounts. *Health Affairs* 24 (6): 1490–1500.

Halm, E. A., C. Lee, and M. R. Chassin. 2002. Is Volume Related to Outcome in Health Care? A Systematic Review and Methodologic Critique of the Literature. *Annals of Internal Medicine* 137 (6): 511–20.

Hansmann, H. 1996. *The Ownership of Enterprise*. Cambridge, Mass.: The Belknap Press of Harvard University Press.

Harley, C., and S. Wagner. 2003. Persistence with COX-2 Inhibitors in Managed Care: An Analysis of Claims Data. *Managed Care Interface* 16 (10): 38–45.

Harris, J. E. 1977. The Internal Organization of Hospitals: Some Economic Implications. *The Bell Journal of Economics* 8 (2): 467–82.

Hart, O. 1995. *Firms, Contracts, and Financial Structure*. New York: Clarendon Press/Oxford Press.

Havighurst, C. C., ed. 1974. *Regulating Health Facilities Construction: Proceedings of a Conference on Health Planning, Certificates of Need, and Market Entry*. Washington, D.C.: AEI Press.

———. 1995. *Health Care Choices: Private Contracts as Instruments of Health Reform*. Washington D.C.: AEI Press.

———. 2000. Freedom of Contract: The Unexplored Path to Health Care Reform. In *American Health Care: Government, Market Processes, and the Public Interest*, ed. R. D. Feldman. New Brunswick: Transaction Publishers.

———. 2005. Monopoly is not the Answer. *Health Affairs* Web Exclusive (August 9): W5-373–75, http://www.healthaffairs.org (accessed May 24, 2006).

Health Care for All—California (2005), Summary of the Single Payer Bill—SB 840, http://www.healthcareforall.org/sb840.html (accessed June 20, 2006).

Heclo, H. 1977. Political Executives and Washington Bureaucracy. *Political Science Quarterly* 92 (3): 395–424.

———. 1979. Issue Networks and the Executive Establishment. In *The New American Political System*, ed. A. King. Washington, D.C.: AEI Press.

Hemingway, H., A. Crook, G. Feder, J. Dawson, and A. Timmins. 2000. Waiting for Coronary Angiography: Is There a Clinically Ordered Queue? *Lancet* 355 (9208): 985–86.

Hensley, S. 2005. Some Drug Makers Are Starting to Curtail TV Ad Spending. *Wall Street Journal*, May 16, B1.

Herzlinger, R. E. 1997. *Market-Driven Healthcare: Who Wins, Who Loses in the Transformation of America's Largest Service Industry*. New York: Perseus Books Group.

————. 2004a. Consumer-Driven Health Care. *Healthcare Financial Management* 53 (3): 66–68.

————. 2004b. Specialization and Its Discontents: The Pernicious Impact of Regulations Against Specialization and Physician Ownership on the U.S. Healthcare System. *Circulation* 109 (20): 2376–78.

————. 2004c. Why We Need Consumer-Driven Health Care. In *Consumer-Driven Health Care: Implications for Providers, Payers, and Policymakers*, ed. R. E. Herzlinger. San Francisco: John Wiley and Sons.

Hill, A. B. 1958. The Experimental Approach in Preventative Medicine. I. The Problems of Experiments in Man. *Journal of the Royal Institute for Public Health and Hygiene* 21 (7): 177–85.

Hill, C. W. L. 1994. Diversification and Economic Performance: Bringing Structure and Corporate Management Back into the Picture. In *Fundamental Issues in Strategy: A Research Agenda*, ed. R. P. Rumelt, D. E. Schendel, and D. J. Teece. Boston, Mass.: Harvard Business School Press.

Hillner, B. E., T. J. Smith, and C. E. Desch. 2000. Hospital and Physician Volume or Specialization and Outcomes in Cancer Treatment: Importance in Quality of Cancer Care. *Journal of Clinical Oncology* 18 (11): 2327–40.

Hoffer Gittell, J. 2004. Achieving Focus in Hospital Care: The Role of Relational Coordination. In *Consumer-Driven Health Care: Implications for Providers, Payers, and Policymakers*, ed. R. E. Herzlinger. San Francisco: John Wiley and Sons.

Hollon, M. F. 1999. Direct-to-Consumer Marketing of Prescription Drugs. *Journal of the American Medical Association* 281 (4): 382–84.

Horwitz, J. R. 2005. Does Corporate Ownership Matter? Service Provision in the Hospital Industry: NBER Working Paper No. 1376. Cambridge, Mass.: National Bureau of Economic Research.

Hsiao, C. 1986. *Analysis of Panel Data*. New York: Cambridge University Press.

Hughes, D., and L. Griffiths. 1997. "Ruling In" and "Ruling Out": Two Approaches to the Micro-Rationing of Health Care. *Social Science and Medicine* 44 (5): 589–99.

Hughes, R. G., D. W. Garnick, Luft H. S., S. J. McPhee, and S. S. Hunt. 1988. Hospital Volume and Patient Outcomes: The Case of Hip Fracture Patients. *Medical Care* 26 (11): 1057–67.

Huh, J., and B. J. Cude. 2004. Is the Information "Fair and Balanced" in Direct-to-Consumer Prescription Drug Websites? *Journal of Health Communication* 9 (6): 529–40.

Hussey, P. S., G. F. Anderson, R. Osborn, C. Feek, V. McLaughlin, J. Millar, and A. Epstein. 2004. How Does the Quality of Care Compare in Five Countries? *Health Affairs* 23 (3): 89–99.

Hyland, T. 2005. Budget Deal Includes Extension of Present Limitations on Specialty Hospitals. *Kaiser Health Care Daily Report* 10 (243).

Iezzoni, L. I. 2003. Range of Risk Factors. In *Risk Adjustment for Measuring Health Care Outcomes*, ed. L. I. Iezzoni. Chicago, Ill.: Health Administration Press.

Iglehart, J. K. 2005. The Emergence of Physician-Owned Specialty Hospitals. *New England Journal of Medicine* 352 (1): 78–84.

Illinois Attorney General. 2006. Madigan Proposes Two Bills to Hold Hospitals Accountable for Charity Care, Stop Unfair Billing and Collection Practices. Press release, January 23. Chicago, Ill.: State of Illinois, http://www.ag.state.il.us/pressroom/2006_01/20060123.html (accessed June 5, 2006).

IMS Health. 2003. Total U.S. Promotional Spend by Type [1996-2002]. Integrated Promotional Services™ and CMR. http://www.imshealth.com/ims/portal/front/articleC/0,2777,6599_41551570_41718516,00.html (accessed June 20, 2006).

———. 2004. Leading 20 Products by U.S. Sales, 2003. IMS National Sales Perspectives™. http://www.imshealth.com/ims/portal/front/articleC/0,2777,6599_42720942_44304277,00.html (accessed June 20, 2006).

———. 2005a. Leading 20 Products by U.S. Sales, 2004. IMS National Sales Perspectives™. http://www.imshealth.com/ims/portal/front/articleC/0,2777,6599_z49695983_69890133,00.html (accessed June 20, 2006).

———. 2005b. Leading 10 Products by U.S. Promotional Dollars, 2004. Integrated Promotional Services™.http://www.imshealth.com/ims/portal/front/articleC/0,2777,6599_49695992_70328475,00.html.

———. 2006a. Leading 20 Products by U.S. Sales, 2005. IMS National Sales Perspectives™. http://www.imshealth.com/ims/portal/front/articleC/0,2777,6599_73915261_77140545,00.html (accessed June 20, 2006).

———. 2006b. Total U.S. Promotional Spend by Type [2001-2005]. Integrated Promotional Services™ and CMR. http://www.imshealth.com/ims/portal/front/articleC/0,2777,6599_78084568_78152318,00.html (accessed June 20, 2006).

Institute of Medicine. 1974. Health Maintenance Organizations: Toward a Fair Market Test. In *Health Care Law and Policy*, ed. C. Havighurst. Westbury, N.Y.: Foundation Press.

International Agency for Research on Cancer. 2003. *Survival of Cancer Patients in Europe: The EUROCARE-2 Study, 1999.* International Agency for Research on Cancer. Lyon, France: IARCPress.

Iqbal, Y., and D. Taylor. 2001. Surgical Hospitals: Where Do They Fit In? *Outpatient Surgery* 11 (7): 6–12.

Jensen, G. A., and M. A. Morrisey. 1999. Employer-Sponsored Health Insurance and Mandated Benefit Laws. *Milbank Quarterly* 77 (4): 425–59.

Johnson, J. A., and A. J. Christensen. 2004. Perceived Control, Desire for Control, and Adherence to a Chronic Medical Regime. *Annals of Behavioral Medicine* 27 (3): 155–61.

Jorgensen, N. E., and T. P. Weil. 1998. Regulating Managed Care Plans: Is the Telecommunications Industry a Possible Model? *Managed Care Quarterly* 6 (3): 7–16.

Joskow, P. L. 1991. The Role of Transaction Cost Economics in Antitrust and Public Utility Regulatory Policies. *Journal of Law, Economics, and Organizations* 7 (Special Issue): 53–83.

————. 1997. Restructuring, Competition, and Regulatory Reform in the U.S. Electricity Sector. *Journal of Economic Perspectives* 11 (3): 119–38.

Joskow, P. L., and N. Rose. 1989. The Effects of Economic Regulation. In *Handbook of Industrial Organization*, vol. 2, ed. R. Schmalensee and R. Willig. New York: Elsevier Science Publishers B.V.

Judis, J. B. 2006. Arnold's Dilemma. *California Magazine* 117 (1): 20–25.

Kahn, C. N. 2006. Intolerable Risk, Irreparable Harm: The Legacy of Physician-Owned Specialty Hospitals. *Health Affairs* 25 (1):130–33.

Kahn, J. G., R. Kronick, M. Kreger, and D. N. Gans. 2005. The Cost of Health Insurance Administration in California: Estimates for Insurers, Physicians, and Hospitals. *Health Affairs* 24 (6): 1629–39.

Kaiser Family Foundation. 2004a. *Employer Health Benefits 2004 Annual Survey*. Menlo Park, Calif., and Chicago, Ill.: Henry J. Kaiser Family Foundation and the Health Research and Educational Trust.

————. 2004b. *The Uninsured: A Primer*. Menlo Park, Calif.: Kaiser Family Foundation, Commission on Medicaid and the Uninsured.

Kane, N. M., and W. H. Wubbenhorst. 2000. Alternative Funding Policies for the Uninsured: Exploring the Value of Hospital Tax Exemption. *Milbank Quarterly* 78 (2): 185–212.

Kaphingst, K. A., W. DeJong, R. E. Rudd, and L. H. Daltroy. 2004. A Content Analysis of Direct-to-Consumer Television Prescription Drug Advertisements. *Journal of Health Communication* 9 (6): 515–28.

Kassirer, J. P. 2004. *On The Take: How Medicine's Complicity with Big Business Can Endanger Your Health*. New York: Oxford University Press.

Kearney, P. M., C. Biagent, J. Godwin, H. Halls, J. R. Emberson, and C. Patrono. 2006. Do Selective Cyclo-Oxygenase-2 Inhibitors and Traditional Non-Steroidal Anti-Inflammatory Drugs Increase the Risk of Atherothrombosis? A Meta-Analysis of Randomized Trials. *British Medical Journal* 332 (7553): 1302–8.

Keating, M. 2004. Health Care Expenses Are a Major Factor in Site Selection Process. *Expansion Management* 19 (2): 18. Available at http://www.expansionmanagement.com/smo/articleviewer/default.asp?cmd=articledetail&articleid=16000&st=2 (accessed May 24, 2006).

Keeler, T. E. 1984. Theories of Regulation and the Deregulation Movement. *Public Choice* 44 (1): 103–45.

————. 1991. Airline Deregulation and Market Performance: The Economic Basis for Regulatory Reform and Lessons from the U.S. Experience. In *Transport in a Free Market Economy*, ed. K. Button. London: Macmillan Academic and Professional Ltd.

Keeler, T. E., and J. S. Ying. 1996. Hospital Costs and Excess Bed Capacity: A Statistical Analysis. *Review of Economics and Statistics* 78 (3): 470–81.

Kenkel, D. S. 1994. The Demand for Preventive Medical Care. *Applied Economics* 26 (4): 313–25.

———. 2000. Prevention. In *Handbook of Health Economics*, ed. A. J. Culyer and J. P. Newhouse. New York: Elsevier Science Publishers B.V.

Kessler, D. P., and J. J. Geppert. 2005. The Effects of Competition on Variation in the Quality and Cost of Medical Care. *Journal of Economics and Management Strategy* 14 (3): 575–89.

Kessler, D. P., and M. B. McClellan. 1996. Do Doctors Practice Defensive Medicine? *Quarterly Journal of Economics* 111 (2): 353–90.

———. 2000. Is Hospital Competition Socially Wasteful? *Quarterly Journal of Economics* 115 (2): 577–615.

——— 2002. The Effects of Hospital Ownership on Medical Productivity. *RAND Journal of Economics* 33 (3): 488–506.

Kleinke, J. D. 2001. *Oxymorons: The Myth of a U.S. Health Care System.* San Francisco: Jossey-Bass.

Klerman, J. A., J. S. Ringel, and B. Roth. 2005. *Under-Reporting of Medicaid and Welfare in the Current Population Survey.* Santa Monica, Calif.: The RAND Corporation.

Korobkin, R. 1999. The Efficiency of Managed Care "Patient Protection" Laws: Incomplete Contracts, Bounded Rationality, and Market Failure. *Cornell Law Review* 85 (1): 1–88.

Kotlikoff, L. J., and C. Hagist. 2005. Who's Going Broke? Comparing Healthcare Costs in Ten OECD Countries. NBER Working Paper No. 11833. Cambridge, Mass.: National Bureau of Economic Research.

Kouri, B. E., R. G. Parsons, and H. R. Alpert. 2002. Physician Self-Referral for Diagnostic Imaging: Review of the Empiric Literature. *American Journal of Roentgenology* 179 (4): 843–50.

Kovner, C., C. Jones, C. Zhan, P. J. Gergen, and J. Basu. 2002. Nurse Staffing and Postsurgical Adverse Events: An Analysis of Administrative Data from a Sample of U.S. Hospitals, 1990–1996. *Health Services Research* 37 (3): 611–29.

Kravitz, R. L., R. M. Epstein, M. D. Feldman, C. E. Franz, R. Azari, M. S. Wilkes, L. Hinton, and P. Franks. 2005. Influence of Patients' Requests for Direct-to-Consumer Advertised Antidepressants: A Randomized Controlled Trial. *Journal of the American Medical Association* 293 (16): 1995–2002.

Kronick, R., and T. Gilmer. 1999. Explaining the Decline in Health Insurance Coverage, 1979–1995. *Health Affairs* 18 (2): 30–47.

Kumbhakar, S. C. 1996. A Parametric Approach to Efficiency Measurement Using a Flexible Profit Function. *Southern Economic Journal* 63 (2): 473–88.

Lang, T. A., M. Hodge, V. Olson, P. S. Romano, and R. L. Kravitz. 2004. Nurse-Patient Ratios: A Systematic Review of the Effects of Nurse Staffing on Patient, Nurse Employee, and Hospital Outcomes. *Journal of Nursing Administration* 34 (7–8): 326–37.

Lanning, J. A., M. A. Morrisey, and R. L. Ohsfeldt. 1991. Endogenous Hospital Regulation and Its Effects on Hospital and Non-Hospital Expenditures. *Journal of Regulatory Economics* 2 (3): 137–54.

Lansky, D. 2002. Improving Quality Through Public Disclosure of Performance Information. *Health Affairs* 21 (4): 52–62.

Leapfrog Group. 2006. Fact Sheet. (http://www.leapfroggroup.org/media/file/LF_FactSheet_01_26_06.pdf, accessed June 22, 2006).

Legislative Council of California. Official California Legislative Information. http://www.leginfo.ca.gov.

Leung, G. M. 2000. Hospitals Must Become "Focused Factories." *British Medical Journal* 320 (7239): 942–43.

Levi, L., M. Michaelson, H. Admi, D. Bregman, and R. Bar-Nahor. 2002. National Strategy for Mass Casualty Situations and its Effects on the Hospital. *Prehospital and Disaster Medicine* 17 (1): 12–16.

Levinthal, D. A. 1996. Organizational Adaptation and Environmental Selection: Interrelated Processes of Change. In *Organizational Learning*, ed. M. D. Cohen and L. S. Sproull. Thousand Oaks, Calif.: SAGE Publications.

Lewin, M. E., and S. Altman. 2000. *America's Health Care Safety Net: Intact but Endangered*. Washington, D.C.: National Academy Press.

Li, T., and R. Rosenman. 2001a. Cost Inefficiency in Washington Hospitals: A Stochastic Frontier Approach Using Panel Data. *Health Care Management Science* 4 (2): 73–81.

————. 2001b. Estimating Hospital Costs with a Generalized Leontief Function. *Health Economics* 10 (6): 523–38.

Lichtenberg, F. R. 2001. Are the Benefits of Newer Drugs Worth Their Cost? Evidence From the 1996 MEPS. *Health Affairs* 20 (5): 241–51.

————. 2003. Pharmaceutical Innovation, Mortality Reduction, and Economic Growth. In *Measuring the Gains from Medical Research: An Economic Approach*, ed. K. M. Murphy and R. H. Topel. Chicago: University of Chicago Press.

Light, D. W. 2003. Universal Health Care: Lessons From the British Experience. *American Journal of Public Health* 93 (1): 25–30.

Llewellyn-Thomas, H., E. Theil, M. Paterson, and C. D. Naylor. 1999. In the Queue for Coronary Artery Bypass Grafting: Patients' Perceptions of Risk and "Maximal Acceptable Waiting Time." *Journal of Health Services, Research, and Policy* 4 (2): 65–72.

Lo Sasso, A. T., T. Rice, J. R. Gabel, and H. Whitmore. 2004. Tales From the New Frontier: Pioneers' Experiences with Consumer-Driven Health Care. *Health Services Research* 39 (4 pt. 2): 1071–90.

Luft, H. S. 1980. The Relation Between Surgical Volume and Mortality: An Exploration of Causal Factors and Alternative Models. *Medical Care* 18 (9): 940–59.

Luft, H. S., S. S. Hunt, and S. C. Maerki. 1987. The Volume-Outcome Relationship: Practice-Makes-Perfect or Selective-Referral Patterns? *Health Services Research* 22 (2): 157–82.

Lyles, A. 2002. Direct Marketing of Pharmaceuticals to Consumers. *Annual Review of Public Health* 23: 73–91.

Lynk, W. J., and C. S. Longley. 2002. The Effect of Physician-Owned Surgicenters on Hospital Outpatient Surgery. *Health Affairs* 21 (4): 215–21.

Magid, D. J., B. N. Calonge, J. S. Rumsfeld, J. G. Canto, P. D. Fenderick, N. R. Every, and H. V. Barron. 2000. Relationship between Hospital Primary Angioplasty Volume and Mortality for Patients with Acute MI Treated with Primary Angioplasty vs. Thrombolytic Therapy. *Journal of the American Medical Association* 284 (24): 3131–38.

Manning, R. L., and A. Keith. 2001. The Economics of Direct-to-Consumer Advertising of Prescription Drugs. *Economic Realities in Health Care* 2 (1): 3–9.

March, J. G. 1996. Exploration and Exploitation in Organizational Learning. In *Organizational Learning*, ed. M. D. Cohen and L. S. Sproull. Thousand Oaks, Calif.: Sage.

Mark, B. A., D. W. Harless, M. McCue, and Y. Xu. 2004. A Longitudinal Examination of Hospital Registered Nurse Staffing and Quality of Care. *Health Services Research* 39 (2): 279–300.

McGinnis, J. M., and W. H. Foege. 1993. Actual Causes of Death in the United States. *Journal of the American Medical Association* 270 (18): 2207–13.

MedCath Corporation. 2006. MedCath Corporate Profile, http://phx.corporate-ir.net/phoenix.zhtml?c=129804&p=irol-homeProfile (accessed May 17, 2006).

MedPAC. 2003a. Transcript from Public Meeting on Inpatient and Outpatient Hospital Payment Issues. Washington, D.C.: Medicare Payment Advisory Commission.

———. 2003b. Accounting for Variation in Hospital Financial Performance Under Prospective Payment. In *Report to Congress: Variation and Innovation in Medicare*. Washington, D.C.: Medicare Policy Advisory Commission.

Menke, T. J. 1997. The Effect of Chain Membership on Hospital Costs. *Health Services Research* 32 (2): 177–97.

Mezei, G., and F. Chung. 1999. Return Hospital Visits and Hospital Readmission After Ambulatory Surgery. *Annals of Surgery* 230 (5): 721–27.

Michigan Department of Community Health. 2003. *Evaluation of Certificate of Need in Michigan*. Vol. 3, *Technical Appendices*. By C. J. Conover and F. A. Sloan. Lansing, Mich.: State of Michigan.

Milgrom, P., and J. Roberts. 1990. Bargaining Costs, Influence Costs, and the Organization of Economic Activity. In *Perspectives on Positive Political Economy*, ed. J. Alt and K. Shepsle. Cambridge: Cambridge University Press

———. 1992. *Economics, Organization and Management*. Englewood Cliffs, N.J.: Prentice Hall.

Miller, R. D., and T. E. Frech. 2004. *Health Care Matters: Pharmaceuticals, Obesity and the Quality of Life*. Washington, D.C.: AEI Press.

Miller, R. H., and H. S. Luft. 1997. Does Managed Care Lead to Better or Worse Quality of Care? *Health Affairs* 16 (1): 7–25.

————. 2002. HMO Plan Performance Update: An Analysis of the Literature, 1997–2001. *Health Affairs* 21 (4): 63–86.

Millstein, L. G. 2003. Prescription Drug Advertising: Is It a Driving Force on Drug Pricing? *North Carolina Medical Journal* 64 (6): 289–91.

Mitchell, J. A., and T. D. Warner. 2006. COX Isoforms in the Cardiovascular System: Understanding the Activities of Non-Steroidal Anti-Inflammatory Drugs. *Nature Reviews Drug Discovery* 5 (1): 75–86.

Mitchell, J. M., and T. R. Sass. 1995. Physician Ownership of Ancillary Services: Indirect Demand Inducement or Quality Assurance? *Journal of Health Economics* 14 (3): 263–89.

Mobley, L. R., and W. D. Bradford. 1997. Behavioral Differences among Hospitals: Is It Ownership, or Location? *Applied Economics* 29 (9): 1125–38.

Mobley, L. R., and T. E. Frech. 1998. Managed Care, Distance Traveled, and Hospital Market Definition. Paper presented at the annual meeting of the American Economics Association, Chicago, Ill., January 4, 1998.

Moe, T. M. 1990. Political Institutions: The Neglected Side of the Story. *Journal of Law, Economics, and Organizations* 6 (Special Issue): 213–53.

————. 1991. Politics and the Theory of Organization. *Journal of Law Economics and Organization* 7 (Special Issue): 106–29.

Moore, N. J. 2003. Regulating Self-Referrals and Other Physician Conflicts of Interest. *HEC Forum* 15 (2): 134–54.

Moore, W. B. 1990. Hospitals Win Healthy Margins by Following Business Basics. *Hospitals*, April 20, 56, 58.

Morrisey, M. A. 1994. *Cost Shifting in Health Care: Separating Evidence from Rhetoric*. Washington, D.C.: AEI Press.

————. 2000. State Health Care Reform: Protecting the Provider. In *American Health Care: Government, Market Processes, and the Public Interest*, ed. R. D. Feldman. New Brunswick, N.J.: Transaction.

Morrisey, M. A., M. L. Kilgore, and L. J. Nelson. 2006. Medical Malpractice Reform and Employer Sponsored Health Insurance Premiums. *Inquiry* (forthcoming).

Morrison, S. A., and C. Winston. 1986. *The Economic Effects of Airline Deregulation*. Washington, D.C.: Brookings Institution.

————. 1995. *The Evolution of the Airline Industry*. Washington D.C.: Brookings Institution.

Morse, S. S. 2002. The Vigilance Defense. *Scientific American*, October, 88–89.

Mueller, R. M. 2001. *As Sick As It Gets: The Shocking Reality of America's Healthcare*. Dunkirk, N.Y.: Olin Frederick.

Myers, H. 1998. Focused Factories: Are You Ready for the Competition? *Hospitals and Health Networks* 72 (7): 24–26, 28–30.

National Institute for Health Care Management Foundation. 2001. *Prescription Drugs and Mass Media Advertising, 2000*. Washington, D.C.: NIHCM Foundation, November.

Naylor, C. D., A. Basinski, R. Baigrie, B. Goldman, and J. Lomas. 1990. Placing Patients in a Queue for Coronary Revascularization: Evidence for Practice Variations from an Expert Panel Process. *American Journal of Public Health* 80 (10): 1246–52.

Naylor, C. D., and C. M. Levinton. 1993. Sex-Related Differences in Coronary Revascularization Practices: The Perspective from a Canadian Queue Management Project. *Canadian Medical Association Journal* 149 (7): 965–73.

Naylor, C. D., C. M. Levinton, R. Baigrie, and B. Goldman. 1992. Placing Patients in the Queue for Coronary Surgery: Do Age and Work Status Alter Canadian Specialists' Decisions? *Journal of General Internal Medicine* 7 (5): 492–98.

Naylor, C. D., C. M. Levinton, S. Wheeler, and L. Hunter. 1993. Queuing for Coronary Surgery During Severe Supply-Demand Mismatch in a Canadian Referral Centre: A Case Study of Implicit Rationing. *Social Science and Medicine* 37 (1): 61–67.

Naylor, C. D., K. Sykora, S. Jaglai, and S. Jefferson. 1995. Waiting for Coronary Artery Bypass Surgery: Population-Based Study of 8517 Consecutive Patients in Ontario, Canada. *Lancet* 346 (8990): 1605-9.

NDCHealth. 2006. The Top 200 Prescriptions for 2004 by U.S. Sales ($billions). Data furnished by NDCHealth. Available at http://www.rxlist.com/top200_sales_2004.htm (accessed June 1, 2006).

Nelson, P. 1974. Advertising as Information. *Journal of Political Economy* 81 (4): 729–54.

Nelson, R. R., and S. G. Winter. 1982. *An Evolutionary Theory of Economic Change.* Cambridge, Mass.: Belknap Press.

New York Times. 2005. Punishment for Merck. August 23.

Newberry, D. M. 1999. *Privatization, Restructuring, and Regulation of Network Utilities.* Cambridge, Mass.: MIT Press.

Nicholson, S. 2002. Physician Specialty Choice Under Uncertainty. *Journal of Labor Economics* 20 (2): 816–47.

Noble, A., and T. A. Brennan. 1999. The Stages of Managed Care Regulation: Developing Better Rules. *Journal of Health Politics, Policy, and Law* 24 (6): 1275–1305.

Noether, M. G. 2000. The Cost of Physician Antitrust Waivers: Updated National Projections. Washington, D.C.: Charles River Associates.

Nooteboom, B. 2000. *Learning and Innovation in Organizations and Economies.* Oxford and New York: Oxford University Press.

Nyman, J. A. 2004. Is "Moral Hazard" Inefficient? The Policy Implications of a New Theory. *Health Affairs* 23 (5): 194–99.

Oberholzer-Gee, F., and S. N. Inarndar. 2004. Merck's Recall of Rofecoxib—A Strategic Perspective. *New England Journal of Medicine* 351 (21): 2147–49.

O'Donnell, K. P. 1993. No More "Business as Usual" for Hospitals. *H&HN: Hospitals & Health Networks* 67 (12): 68.

Ohsfeldt, R. L. 2004. If the "Business Model" of Medicine is Sick, What's the Diagnosis, and What's the Cure? *Independent Review* 8 (2): 271–83.

Ohsfeldt, R. L., M. J. Lage, and K. Rajagopalan. 2005. Patterns of Treatment for Bipolar Disorder. In working paper, University of Iowa, Iowa City.

Ohsfeldt, R. L., M. Morrisey, L. J. Nelson, and V. Johnson. 1998. The Spread of State "Any Willing Provider" Laws. *Health Services Research* 33 (5, pt. 2): 1537–62.

Organization for Economic Cooperation and Development. 2003. *OECD Health Data 2003* (CD-ROM). New Milford, Conn.: OECD Publishing.

———. 2006. *OECD Factbook 2006: Economic, Environmental and Social Statistics.* http://caliban.sourceoecd.org/vl=3361198/cl=22/nw=1/rpsv/factbook/data/02-01-01-t02.xls (accessed June 20, 2006).

Owen, B. M. 1985. Interest Groups and the Political Economy of Regulation. In *Incentives vs. Controls in Health Policy: Broadening the Debate*, ed. J. A. Meyer. Washington, D.C.: AEI Press.

Pacific Business Group on Health. 2006. Mission and Goals. http://www.pbgh.org/about_pbgh/mission_and_goals.asp (accessed June 20, 2006).

Palumbo, F. B., and C. D. Mullins. 2002. The Development of Direct-to-Consumer Prescription Drug Advertising Regulation. *Food and Drug Law Journal* 57 (3): 423–43.

Panel on the Nonprofit Sector. 2005. Strengthening Transparency Governance Accountability of Charitable Organizations. In *Final Report to Congress*. Washington, D.C.: Independent Sector.

Panzar, J. C., and R. D. Willig. 1981. Economies of Scope. *American Economic Review* 71 (2): 268–72.

Patel, K., and M. E. Rushefsky. 2002. The Canadian Health Care System. In *Handbook of International Health Care Systems*, ed. K. V. Thai, E. T. Wimberley, and S. M. McManus. New York: Marcel Dekker.

Pauly, M. V. 2005. Competition and New Technology. *Health Affairs* 24 (6): 1523–35.

Pauly, M. V., and M. L. Berger. 1999. Why Should Managed Care be Regulated? In *Regulating Managed Care*, ed. S. H. Altman, U. E. Reinhardt, and D. Shactman. San Francisco: Jossey-Bass.

Pauly, M. V., and L. M. Nichols. 2004. Ten Myths of the Uninsured. *AHIP Coverage*, May/June, http://www.ahip.org/content/default.aspx?bc=31|130|136|400|401 (accessed May 24, 2006).

Pauly, M. V., and S. Nicholson. 1999. Adverse Consequences of Adverse Selection. *Journal of Health Politics, Policy and Law* 24 (5): 921–30.

Payton, S., and R. Powsner. 1980. Regulation Through the Looking Glass: Hospitals, Blue Cross, and Certificate of Need. *Michigan Law Review* 79: 203–77.

Peltzman, S. 1976. Toward a More General Theory of Regulation. *Journal of Law and Economics* 19: 211–40.

Peltzman, S., and C. Winston. 2000. *Deregulation of Network Industries: What's Next.* Washington, D.C.: AEI-Brookings Joint Center for Regulatory Studies.

Peterson, C. L., and A. Grady. 2005. *Medicaid/SCHIP Enrollees: Comparison of Counts from Administrative Data and Survey Estimates.* Washington, D.C.: Congressional Research Service.

Pignone, M., S. Saha, T. Hoerger, and J. Mandelblatt. 2002. Cost-Effectiveness Analyses of Colorectal Cancer Screening: A Systematic Review for the U.S. Preventive Services Task Force. *Annals of Internal Medicine* 137 (2): E96–106.

Pines, W. L. 1999. A History and Perspective on Direct to Consumer Promotion. *Food and Drug Law Journal* 54 (3): 489–518.

Porter, E. 2004. Rising Cost of Health Benefits Cited as Factor in Slump of Jobs. *New York Times*, August 19.

Porter, M. F., and F. O. Teisberg. 2004. Refining Competition in Health Care. *Harvard Business Review* 82 (6): 65–76.

Priest, G. 1993. The Origins of Utility Regulation and the Theories of Regulation Debate. *Journal of Law and Economics* 36: 289–329.

Relman, A. S., and U. E. Reinhardt. 1986. Debating For-Profit Health Care and the Ethics of Physicians. *Health Affairs* 5 (2): 5–31.

Reschovsky, J. D., and P. Kemper. 2000. Do HMOs Make a Difference? *Inquiry* 36 (4): 374–77.

Rice, T. 1998. *The Economics of Health Reconsidered.* Chicago, Ill.: Health Administration Press.

Robinson, A. R., K. B. Hohmann, J. I. Rifkin, D. Topp, C. M. Gilroy, J. A. Pickard, and R. J. Anderson. 2004. Direct-to-Consumer Pharmaceutical Advertising: Physician and Public Opinion and Potential Effects on the Physician-Patient Relationship. *Archives of Internal Medicine* 164 (4): 427–32.

Robinson, J. C. 1997. Use and Abuse of the Medical Loss Ratio to Measure Health Plan Performance. *Health Affairs* 16 (4): 176–87.

———. 1999. *The Corporate Practice of Medicine: Competition and Innovation in Health Care.* Berkeley, Calif.: University of California Press.

———. 2001. The End of Asymmetric Information. *Journal of Health Politics, Policy and Law* 26 (5): 1045–53.

———. 2005. Entrepreneurial Challenges to Integrated Health Care. In *Policy Challenges in Modern Health Care*, ed. D. Mechanic, L. B. Rogut, D. C. Colby, and J. R. Knickman. New Brunswick, N.J.: Rutgers University Press.

Rogal, D., and R. Stenger. 2001. *The Challenge of Managed Care Regulation: Making Markets Work?* Washington, D.C.: Academy for Health Services Research and Health Policy.

Rohack, J. J. 2004. Report to the Board of Trustees: Specialty Hospitals and Impact on Health Care. Chicago, Ill.: American Medical Association.

Romano, M. 2005. Buying Into Practices. *Modern Healthcare* 35 (24): 4.

Romano, M., and B. Kirchheimer. 2001. The Latest Surgery Suite, and a Room with a View. *Modern Healthcare* 31 (9): 26–28, 30.

Rosenberg, C. E. 1987. *In the Care of Strangers: The Rise of the American Hospital System*. New York: Basic Books.

Rosenthal, M. B., E. R. Berndt, J. M. Donohue, R. G. Frank, and A. M. Epstein. 2002. Promotion of Prescription Drugs to Consumers. *New England Journal of Medicine* 346 (7): 498–505.

Roth, D., and D. Kelch. 2001. *Making Sense of Managed Care Regulation in California*. Oakland, Calif.: California Health Care Foundation.

Rozek, R. P. 1988. A Nonparametric Test for Economies of Scope. *Applied Economics* 20: 653–63.

Salkever, D. S., and T. W. Bice. 1979. *Hospital Certificate-of-Need Controls: Impact on Investment, Costs, and Use*. Washington, D.C.: AEI Press.

Santerre, R. E., and J. A. Vernon. 2005. Hospital Ownership Mix Efficiency in the US: An Exploratory Study. NBER Working Paper No. 11192. Cambridge, Mass.: National Bureau of Economic Research.

Schmalensee, R. 1978. A Model of Advertising and Product Quality. *Journal of Political Economy* 86 (3): 485–503.

Schneider, J. E. 1999. Cost Estimates of Pending California Managed Care Reform Legislation. Sacramento, Calif.: California Association of Health Plans.

———. 2003. Changes in the Effects of Mandatory Rate Regulation on Growth in Hospital Operating Costs, 1980–1996. *Review of Industrial Organization* 22 (4): 297–312.

Schneider, J. E., R. L. Ohsfeldt, M. A. Morrisey, B. A. Zelner, and T. R. Miller. 2005. *Economic and Policy Analysis of Specialty Hospitals*. Iowa City, Iowa: Health Economics Consulting Group.

Schneider, J. E., and G. C. Pope. 1992. Trends in Physician Income. *Health Affairs* 11 (1): 181–93.

Schoen, C., M. M. Doty, S. R. Collins, L. Alyssa, and A. L. Holmgren. 2005a. Insured But Not Protected: How Many Adults are Underinsured? *Health Affairs* Web Exclusive (W5): 289–302.

Schoen, C., R. Osborn, P. H. Huynh, and M. Doty. 2005b. Taking the Pulse of Health Care Systems: Experiences of Patients with Health Problems in Six Countries. *Health Affairs* Web Exclusive (November 3): W5-509, http://www. healthaffairs.org (accessed May 24, 2006).

Schur, C., F. Feldman, and L. Zhao. 2004. *The Purchase of Health Insurance by California's Non-Poor Uninsured: How Can It Be Increased?* Oakland, Calif.: California Health Care Foundation.

Schwartz, N. D., and N. Watson. 2003. The Pentagon's Private Army. *Fortune*, March 3, 100–108.

Shactman, David. 2005. Specialty Hospitals, Ambulatory Surgery Centers, and General Hospitals: Charting a Wise Public Policy Course. *Health Affairs* 24 (3): 868–73.

Shahian, D. M., and S. L. Normand. 2003. The Volume Outcome Relationship: From Luft to Leapfrog. *Annals of Thoracic Surgery* 75 (3): 1048–58.

Sheils, J. F., and R. A. Haught. 2005. The Health Care for All Californians Act: Cost and Economic Impacts Analysis. Washington, D.C.: The Lewin Group.

Shen, Y., K. Eggleston, J. Lau, and C. Schmid. 2005. Hospital Ownership and Financial Performance: A Quantitative Research Review. NBER Working Paper No. 11662. Cambridge, Mass.: National Bureau of Economic Research.

Short, P. F. 2000. Hitting a Moving Target: Income-Related Health Insurance Subsidiaries for the Uninsured. *Journal of Policy Analysis and Management* 19 (3): 383–402.

Shortell, S. M., E. Morrison, and S. Hughes. 1989. The Keys to Successful Diversification: Lessons from Leading Hospital Systems. *Hospital and Health Services Administration* 34 (4): 471–92.

Sinay, U. A., and C. R. Campbell. 1995. Scope and Scale Economies in Merging Hospitals Prior to Merger. *Journal of Economics and Finance* 19 (2): 107–23.

Skinner, W. 1974. The Focused Factory. *Harvard Business Review* 52 (3): 113–20.

Sloan, F. A. 1988. Containing Health Expenditures: Lessons Learned from Certificate of Need Programs. In *Cost, Quality, and Access in Health Care: New Roles for Health Planning in a Competitive Environment*, ed. F. A. Sloan. San Francisco: Jossey-Bass.

Sloan, F. A., and M. A. Hall. 2002. Market Failures and the Evolution of State Regulation of Managed Care. *Law and Contemporary Problems* 65:169–94.

Sloan, F. A., G. Picone, D. Taylor, and S. Chou. 2001. Hospital Ownership and Cost and Quality of Care: Is There a Dime's Worth of Difference? *Journal of Health Economics* 20 (1): 1–21.

Sloan, F. A., and B. Steinwald. 1980. Effects of Regulation on Hospital Costs and Input Use. *Journal of Law and Economics* 23 (1): 81–109.

Smith, R. B. 2002. The Return of the Heart Hospital. *Healthcare Financial Management* 56 (10): 76.

Snail, T. S., and J. C. Robinson. 1998. Organizational Diversification in the American Hospital. *Annual Review of Public Health* 19:417–53.

Speidel, R. E. 1993. Article 2 and Relational Sales Contracts. *Loyola of Los Angeles Law Review* 26 (3): 789–809.

Spetz, J., J. A. Seago, J. Coffman, E. Rosenhoff, and E. O'Neil. 2000. *Minimum Nurse Staffing Ratios in California Acute Care Hospitals*. Oakland, Calif.: California HealthCare Foundation.

Stauffer, M. 2000. *State Managed Care Laws 2000: A State-by-State Review*. Washington, D.C.: National Conference of State Legislatures.

Stivers, A., and V. J. Tremblay. 2005. Advertising, Search Costs, and Social Welfare. *Information Economics and Policy* 17 (3): 317–33.

Stout, S. M., and D. C. Warner. 2003. How Did Physician Ownership Become a Federal Case? The Stark Amendments and Their Prospects. *HEC Forum* 15 (2): 171–87.

Strunk, B. C., and J. D. Reschovsky. 2002. Working Families' Health Insurance Coverage, 1997–2001. Tracking Report No. 4. Washington, D.C.: Center for Studying Health System Change.

Studdert, D. M., M. M. Mello, W. M. Sage, C. M. DesRoches, J. Peugh, K. Zapert, and T. A. Brennan. 2005. Defensive Medicine Among High-Risk Specialist Physicians in a Volatile Malpractice Environment. *Journal of the American Medical Association* 293 (21): 2609–17.

Sturm, R. 2002. The Effects of Obesity, Smoking and Drinking on Medical Problems and Costs. *Health Affairs* 21 (2): 245–53.

Teece, D. J., and G. Pisano. 1994. The Dynamic Capabilities of Firms: An Introduction. *Industrial and Corporate Change* 3 (3): 537–56.

Teece, D. J., R. Rumelt, G. Dosi, and S. Winter. 1994. Understanding Corporate Coherence: Theory and Evidence. *Journal of Economic Behavior and Organization* 23: 1–30.

Tengs, T. O., M. E. Adams, J. S. Pliskin, D. G. Safran, J. E. Siegel, M. C. Weinstein, and J. D. Graham. 1995. Five Hundred Life-Saving Interventions and Their Cost-Effectiveness. *Risk Analysis: An International Journal* 15 (3): 369–91.

Thorpe, K. E. 1999. Managed Care as Victim or Villain? *Journal of Health Politics, Policy and Law* 24 (5): 949–56.

Tramer, M. R., R. A. Moore, D. J. M. Reynolds, and H. J. McQuay. 2000. Quantitative Estimation of Rare Adverse Events Which Follow a Biological Progression: A New Model Applied to Chronic NSAID Use. *Pain* 85 (1–2): 169–82.

Tuohy, C. H. 1999. Dynamics of a Changing Health Sphere: The United States, Britain, and Canada. *Health Affairs* 18 (3): 114–34.

———. 2002. The Costs of Constraint and Prospects for Health Care Reform in Canada. *Health Affairs* 21 (3): 32–46.

U.S. Attorney's Office Middle District of Alabama (December 20, 2005), The Special Grand Jury's Continued Probe into Public Corruption Results in Second Superseding Indictment, Press release, http://www.usdoj.gov/usao/alm/Press/siegelman_superceding.html (accessed June 20, 2006).

U.S. Bureau of the Census. 2005a. *Annual Demographic Survey*, March supplement. Washington, D.C.: Government Printing Office.

———. 2005b. *Income, Poverty, and Health Insurance in the United States 2004*. Current Population Reports, P60-299, August. Washington, D.C.: Government Printing Office.

U.S. Bureau of Labor Statistics. 2004. National Compensation Survey. July, www.bls.gov/ncs/home.htm (accessed June 5, 2006).

———. 2006. Consumer Price Index—Urban Consumers - U.S. All Items. Available at http://data.bls.gov/cgi-bin/surveymost?cu (accessed June 26, 2006).

U.S. Congress. Congressional Budget Office. 1999. Cost Estimate: S.6 Patients' Bill of Rights Act of 1999. Washington, D.C.: Government Printing Office.

———. 2003. How Many People Lack Health Insurance and for How Long?: Economic and Budget Issue Brief. Washington, D.C.: Government Printing Office.

U.S. Congress. Congressional Research Service. Domestic Social Policy Division. 2004. Medicare: Physician Self-Referral ("Stark I and II"). By J. O'Sullivan.

http://www.law.umaryland.edu/marshall/crsreports/crsdocuments/RL32494.pdf (accessed May 1, 2006).

U.S. Congress. House of Representatives. Committee on Government Reform. 2005. The Roles of FDA and Pharmaceutical Companies in Ensuring the Safety of Approved Drugs, Like Vioxx. Testimony by J. E. Calfee, 109th Cong., 1st sess. Available at http://www.aei.org/publications/pubID.22465,filter.all/pub_detail.asp (accessed May 1, 2006).

U.S. Congress. House of Representatives. Committee on Ways and Means. Subcommittee on Oversight of the House. 2004. Medical Bad Debt: A Growing Public Health Crisis. Testimony by N. M. Kane, 108th Cong., 2d sess. Washington, D.C.: Government Printing Office.

U.S. Congress. Senate. Committee on Homeland Security and Governmental Affairs. Subcommittee on Federal Financial Management. 2005. Physician-Owned Specialty Hospitals. Testimony by Mark E. Miller, PhD, of Medicare Payment Advisory Commission, 109th Cong., 1st sess. Washington, D.C.: Government Printing Office.

U.S. Department of Commerce. International Trade Administration. 2004. Pharmaceutical Price Controls in OECD Countries: Implications for U.S. Consumers, Pricing, Research and Development, and Innovation. Washington, D.C.: Government Printing Office.

U.S. Department of Health and Human Services. 2004. Area Resource File, 2004 Edition (CD-ROM), Health Resources and Services Administration, Bureau of Health Professions, Rockville, Md.

U.S. Department of Health and Human Services. Agency for Healthcare Research and Quality. 2004. Hospital Nurse Staffing and Quality of Care. By M. W. Stanton and M. K. Rutherford. Research in Action, no. 14 (Pub. No. 04-0029). Washington, D.C.: Government Printing Office.

U.S. Department of Health and Human Services. Centers for Disease Control. National Center for Health Statistics. 2002a. Deaths: Leading Causes for 2000. By R. N. Anderson and B. L. Smith. National Vital Statistics Reports 50 (16): 1–86, available at http://www.cdc.gov/nchs/data/nvsr/nvsr50/nvsr50_16.pdf (accessed June 5, 2006).

———. 2002b. Trends in Racial and Ethnic-Specific Rates for Health Status Indicators: United States 1990–98. By K. G. Keppel, J. N. Percy, and D. K. Wagener. Healthy People Statistical Notes, no. 23 (January), http://www.cdc.gov/nchs/products/pubs/pubd/hp2k/statnt/30-21.htm (accessed May 29, 2006).

———. 2004. United States Life Tables 2001. By E. Arias, National Vital Statistics Reports 52 (14): 1–39, http://www.cdc.gov/nchs/data/nvsr/nvsr52/nvsr52_14.pdf (accessed June 5, 2006).

U.S. Department of Health and Human Services. Centers for Medicare and Medicaid Services. 2005. Study of Physician-Owned Specialty Hospitals Required in Section 507(c)(2) of the Medicare Prescription Drug, Improvement, and Modernization Act of 2003. Washington, D.C.: Government Printing Office.

U.S. Department of Health and Human Services. Office of the Assistant Secretary for Planning and Evaluation. 2003. Addressing the New Health Care Crisis: Reforming the Medical Litigation System to Improve the Quality of Health Care. Washington, D.C.: Government Printing Office.

U.S. Federal Trade Commission and U.S. Department of Justice. 2003. *Health Care Competition Law and Policy*. Washington, D.C.: Government Printing Office.

———. 2004. *Improving Health Care: A Dose of Competition*. Washington, D.C.: Government Printing Office.

U.S. Food and Drug Administration. Center for Drug Evaluation and Research. 2003. *Direct-to-Consumer Advertising of Prescription Drugs: Physician Survey Preliminary Results*. By K. Aikin. Washington, D.C.: Government Printing Office.

———. 2005. *Analysis and Recommendations for Agency Action Regarding Non-Steroidal Anti-Inflammatory Drugs and Cardiovascular Risk*. By J. K. Jenkins and P. J. Seligman. Washington, D.C.: Government Printing Office.

U.S. General Accounting Office. 2003a. Specialty Hospitals: Information on National Market Share, Physician Ownership, and Patients Served. Washington, D.C.: Government Printing Office.

———. 2003b. Specialty Hospitals: Geographic Location, Services Provided, and Financial Performance. Washington, D.C.: General Printing Office.

U.S. National Cancer Institute. 2003. *SEER Cancer Statistics Review, 1975–2000*, http://seer.cancer.gov/csr/1975_2000/index.html (accessed January 16, 2004).

Urquhart, D. J. B., and A. O'Dell. 2004. A Model of Focused Health Care Delivery. In *Consumer-Driven Health Care: Implications for Providers, Payers, and Policymakers*, ed. R. E. Herzlinger. San Francisco: John Wiley and Sons.

Utterbach, J. M. 1994. *Mastering the Dynamics of Innovation*. Boston, Mass.: Harvard Business School Press.

Vaughan-Sarrazin, M. S., E. L. Hannan, C. J. Gormley, and G. E. Rosenthal. 2002. Mortality in Medicare Beneficiaries Following Coronary Artery Bypass Graft Surgery in States With and Without Certificate of Need Regulation. *Journal of the American Medical Association* 288 (15): 1859–66.

Vietor, R. 1994. *Contrived Competition: Regulation and Deregulation in America*. Cambridge, Mass.: Belknap Press.

Vita, M. G. 1990. Exploring Hospital Production Relationships with Flexible Functional Forms. *Journal of Health Economics* 9 (1): 1–21.

Vita, M. G., and S. Sacher. 2001. The Competitive Effects of Not-for-Profit Hospital Mergers: A Case Study. *Journal of Industrial Economics* 49 (1): 63.

Vladeck, B. C. 2006. Paying for Hospitals' Community Service. *Health Affairs* 25 (1): 34–43.

Vogel, R. J., S. Ramachandran, and W. M. Zachry. 2003. A 3-Stage Model for Assessing the Probable Economic Effects of Direct to Consumer Advertising of Pharmaceuticals. *Clinical Therapeutics* 25 (1): 309–29.

Walker, L. R., and M. D. Rosko. 1988. Evaluation of Health Care Service Diversification Options in Health Care Institutions and Programs by Portfolio Analysis: A Marketing Approach. *Journal of Health Care Marketing* 8 (1): 48–59.

Walker, T. 1998. Specialty Care Facilities Make a Case by Improving Outcomes and Costs. *Managed Healthcare* 8 (6): 51–54.

Wall Street Journal. 2006. New England Journal of Politics. January 16, A14.

Walshe, K., and S. M. Shortell. 2004. Social Regulation of Healthcare Organizations in the United States: Developing a Framework for Evaluation. *Health Services Management Research* 17 (2): 79–99.

Warner, M. A., S. E. Shields, and C. G. Chute. 1993. Major Morbidity and Mortality Within 1 Month of Ambulatory Surgery and Anesthesia. *Journal of the American Medical Association* 270 (12): 1437–41.

Weber, R. J., J. A. Showstach, K. A. Hunt, D. C. Colby, and M. L. Callaham. 2005. Does Lack of a Usual Source of Care or Health Insurance Increase the Likelihood of an Emergency Department Visit? Results of a National Population-Based Study. *Annals of Emergency Medicine* 45 (1): 4–12.

Weil, T. P. 1996. How Health Networks and HMOs Could Result in Public Utility Regulation. *Hospital and Health Services Administration* 41 (2): 266–80.

Weinstein, J. N., K. K. Bronner, T. S. Morgan, and J. E. Wennberg. 2004. Trends and Geographic Variations in Major Surgery for Degenerative Diseases of the Hip, Knee, and Spine. *Health Affairs* Web Exclusive (October 7): VAR-81–89, http://www.healthaffairs.org (accessed May 24, 2006).

Weissman, J. S. 2005. The trouble with uncompensated hospital care. *New England Journal of Medicine* 352 (12): 1171–73.

Whitney, S. N., A. L. McGuire, and L. B. McCullough. 2004. A Typology of Shared Decision Making, Informed Consent and Simple Consent. *Annals of Internal Medicine* 140 (1): 54–59.

Whittle, J. R. 2000. COX-1 and COX-2 Products in the Gut; Therapeutic Impact of COX-2 Inhibitors. *Gut* 47 (3): 320–25.

Williamson, O. E. 1985. *The Economics of Institutions of Capitalism: Firms, Markets, Relational Contracting.* New York: Free Press.

———. 1991. Comparative Economic Organization: The Analysis of Discrete Structural Alternatives. *Administrative Science Quarterly* 36 (2): 269–96.

———. 1996. *The Mechanisms of Governance.* New York: Oxford University Press.

———. 1999. Public and Private Bureaucracies: A Transaction Cost Economics Perspective. *Journal of Law, Economics, and Organizations* 15 (1): 306–47.

Wilson, B. C. 2006. My Hospital Was Doomed. *Wall Street Journal*, A20, January 5, 2006.

Wilson, J. Q. 1989. *Bureaucracy: What Government Agencies Do and Why They Do It.* New York: Basic Books/Harper-Collins.

Winston, C. M. 1993. Economic Deregulation: Days of Reckoning for Microeconomists. *Journal of Economic Literature* 31 (3):1263–89.

————. 1998. U.S. Industry Adjustment to Economic Deregulation. *Journal of Economic Perspectives* 12 (3): 89–110.

Winston, C. M., T. M. Corsi, C. M. Grimm, and C. A. Evans. 1990. *The Economic Effects of Surface Freight Deregulation*. Washington, D.C.: Brookings Institution.

Winter, A. 2003. Comparing the Mix of Patients in Various Outpatient Surgery Settings. *Health Affairs* 22 (6): 68–75.

Wolfe, M. M., D. R. Lichtenstein, and G. Singh. 1999. Gastrointestinal Toxicity of Nonsteroidal Antiinflammatory Drugs. *New England Journal of Medicine* 340 (24): 1888–99.

Wolfe, S. M. 2002. Direct-to-Consumer Advertising: Education or Emotion Promotion? *New England Journal of Medicine* 346 (7): 524–26.

Wolski, C. 2004. Watching Your Back. *Orthopedic Technology Review* 6 (6). Available at http://www.orthopedictechreview.com/issues/sepoct04/pg14.htm (accessed May 24, 2006).

Womack, J. P., D. T. Jones, and D. Roos. 1990. *The Machine That Changed the World*. New York: Harper Perennial.

Woolhandler, S., T. Campbell, and D. U. Himmelstein. 2003. Costs of Health Care Administration in the United States and Canada. *New England Journal of Medicine* 349 (8): 768–75.

Woolhandler, S., and D. U. Himmelstein. 1997. Costs of Care and Administration at For-Profit and Other Hospitals in the United States. *New England Journal of Medicine* 336 (11): 769–74.

World Health Organization. 2000. *The World Health Report 2000: Health Systems: Improving Performance*. Geneva, Switzerland: World Health Organization.

————. 2004. *World Health Statistics 2004*, http://www.who.int/healthinfo/en/index.html (accessed June 17, 2004).

Wright, J. R. 1996. *Interest Groups and Congress: Lobbying, Contributions, and Influence*. Boston, Mass.: Allyn and Bacon.

Wruck, K. H., and M. C. Jensen. 1994. Science, Specific Knowledge, and Total Quality Management. *Journal of Accounting and Economics* 18 (3): 247–87.

Younis, M. Z., and D. A. Forgione. 2005. Using Return on Equity and Total Profit Margin to Evaluate Hospital Performance in the U.S.: A Piecewise Regression Analysis. *Journal of Health Care Finance* 31 (3): 82–88.

Zachry, W. M., J. E. Dalen, and T. R. Jackson. 2003. Clinicians' Responses to Direct-to-Consumer Advertising of Prescription Medications. *Archives of Internal Medicine* 163 (15): 1808–12.

Zelman, W. A. 1999. Regulating Managed Care: An Overview. In *Regulating Managed Care*, eds. S. H. Altman, U. E. Reinhardt, and D. Shactman. San Francisco: Jossey-Bass.

Zientek, D. M. 2003. Physician Entrepreneurs, Self-Referral, and Conflicts of Interest: An Overview. *HEC Forum* 15 (2): 111–33.

Zuckerman, A. M. 2004. Competing on Quality. *Hospitals and Health Networks*, June 21, http://www.hhnmag.com/hhnmag/hospitalconnect/search/article. jsp?dcrpath=AHA/PubsNewsArticle/data/040622HHN_Online_Zuckerman& domain=HHNMAG (accessed May 24, 2006).

Index

About the Authors

Robert L. Ohsfeldt is a professor in the Department of Health Policy and Management at the School of Rural Public Health, Texas A&M Health Science Center. He is author or coauthor of more than eighty papers published in peer-reviewed journals and has been the principal investigator for research grants funded by the Agency for Healthcare Research and Quality, National Cancer Institute, Centers for Disease Control, and the Robert Wood Johnson Foundation. Ohsfeldt has served as a peer-reviewer for more than thirty scientific journals and has been a member of grant review panels for the National Institutes of Health, the Agency for Healthcare Research and Quality, and the Department of Veterans Affairs. He also is a member of the editorial board for the *Journal of Managed Care Pharmacy*. Before moving to Texas A&M, Ohsfeldt was a professor in the Department of Health Management and Policy at the University of Iowa. Previously, he was employed as a manager of health outcomes research for Eli Lilly and Company, where he received the President's Award from Lilly Research Laboratories in 2001. Ohsfeldt also has been a research economist with the Center for Health Policy Research at the American Medical Association, an assistant professor in the School of Health Administration and Policy at Arizona State University, and a professor in the Department of Health Care Organization and Policy at the University of Alabama at Birmingham, where he served as interim department chair in 1997. Ohsfeldt completed his doctorate in economics at the University of Houston in 1983, and was a Robert Wood Johnson Foundation Fellow in Healthcare Finance at Johns Hopkins University and the Texas Medical Center during 1987–88.

John E. Schneider is an assistant professor in the Department of Health Management and Policy at the University of Iowa College of Public Health. He also holds secondary appointments in the Department of Economics and the Iowa City VA Center for Research in the Implementation of Innovative Strategies in Practice. His doctorate is in Health Services and Policy Analysis from the University of California, Berkeley. He has over fifteen years of experience studying economic and organizational aspects of the health care industry. Schneider was a research analyst at the Center for Health Economics Research from 1989 to 1993, involved extensively in analyses of large databases, cost analyses, and economic modeling of regulatory programs. Prior to coming to Iowa, he was the director of research at the California Association of Health Plans. His research interests and expertise include health insurance and managed care, regulation, hospital competition, specialty hospitals, economic effects of clinical practice guidelines, insurer-provider contracting, cost-effectiveness analysis, and workplace health promotion. Schneider has served as a consultant to managed care organizations, state health departments, trade associations, and research organizations.